WORLD WAR I AT HOME

PROBLEMS IN AMERICAN HISTORY

EDITOR

LOREN BARITZ

State University of New York, Albany

THE NATURE OF LINCOLN'S LEADERSHIP
Donald E. Fehrenbacher

THE AMERICAN CONSTITUTION
Paul Goodman

THE AMERICAN REVOLUTION
Richard J. Hooker

AMERICA IN THE COLD WAR
Walter LaFeber

ORIGINS OF THE COLD WAR, 1941–1947
Walter LaFeber

AMERICAN IMPERIALISM IN 1898
Richard H. Miller

TENSIONS IN AMERICAN PURITANISM
Richard Reinitz

THE GREAT AWAKENING
Darrett B. Rutman

WORLD WAR I AT HOME
David F. Trask

THE CRITICAL YEARS,
AMERICAN FOREIGN POLICY, 1793–1825
Patrick C. T. White

WORLD WAR I AT HOME

Readings on American Life, 1914-1920

EDITED BY

DAVID F. TRASK

State University of New York at Stony Brook

JOHN WILEY & SONS, INC.

NEW YORK · LONDON · SYDNEY · TORONTO

For IRVING and MARY BROOKS

SERIES PREFACE

This series is an introduction to the most important problems in the writing and study of American history. Some of these problems have been the subject of debate and argument for a long time, although others only recently have been recognized as controversial. However, in every case, the student will find a vital topic, an understanding of which will deepen his knowledge of social change in America.

The scholars who introduce and edit the books in this series are teaching historians who have written history in the same general area as their individual books. Many of them are leading scholars in their fields, and all have done important work in the collective search for better historical understanding.

Because of the talent and the specialized knowledge of the individual editors, a rigid editorial format has not been imposed on them. For example, some of the editors believe that primary source material is necessary to their subjects. Some believe that their material should be arranged to show conflicting interpretations. Others have decided to use the selected materials as evidence for their own interpretations. The individual editors have been given the freedom to handle their books in the way that their own experience and knowledge indicate is best. The overall result is a series built up from the individual decisions of working scholars in the various fields, rather than one that conforms to a uniform editorial decision.

A common goal (rather than a shared technique) is the bridge of this series. There is always the desire to bring the reader as close to these problems as possible. One result of this objective is an emphasis of the nature and consequences of problems and events, with a de-emphasis of the more purely historiographical issues. The goal is to involve the student in the reality of crisis, the inevitability of ambiguity, and the excitement of finding a way through the historical maze.

Above all, this series is designed to show students how experienced historians read and reason. Although health is not contagious, intellectual engagement may be. If we show students something significant in a phrase or a passage that they otherwise may have missed, we will have accomplished part of our objective. When students see something that passed us by, then the process will have been made whole. This active and mutual involvement of editor and reader with a significant human problem will rescue the study of history from the smell and feel of dust.

Loren Baritz

vii

ACKNOWLEDGMENTS

I am pleased to acknowledge the help of four fine research assistants—Emily Rosenberg, Isobel Notturno, Hutch Johnson, and Stephen Pilnick. The editorial assistance of William L. Gum was particularly appreciated. My wife, Elizabeth Brooks Trask, once again contributed her stenographic skill and unfailing optimism.

D.F.T.

Caspian Lake
Greensboro, Vermont

CONTENTS

Introduction   1

PART I.   NEUTRALITY, 1914–1917   19

INITIAL SHOCK   21

1. *William Howard Taft,* "A Message to the People
    of the United States.   21

2. "Mental Unpreparedness."   25

3. *Thomas W. Lamont,* "Financial Illusions of the War."   30

4. "The War-Boom Town in America."   36

PACIFICISM AND PREPAREDNESS   39

5. *Jane Addams,* "What War Is Destroying."   39

6. "Was Jesus Christ a Pacifist?"   42

7. *Paul U. Kellogg,* "A Bill of Particulars: Items in an
    International Policy for America."   45

8. *John Hays Hammond,* "The Issues of 1916."   49

9. *John Grier Hibben,* "The Colleges and National
    Defense."   55

10. *Robert Cromwell Root,* "Military Training in Schools:
    Twelve Objections."   59

ONSET OF BELIGERENCY   62

11. *Sydney Brooks,* "Impressions of America at War."   62

12. "For Freedom and Democracy."   66

13. *Norman Thomas,* et. al., "The Religion of Free Men."   69

14. *Randolph Bourne,* "The War and the Intellectuals."   73

PART II. BELLIGERENCY, 1917–1918   81

MOBILIZATION   83

15. *Louise Maunsell Field,* "Sentimentalizing Over
    the Hun."   83
16. *Lee Simonson,* "Mobilizing the Billboards."   86
17. *Florence Woolston,* "Billy and the World War."   89
18. *Walter S. Gifford,* "A National Picture Puzzle."   95
19. "America's Food Problem."   98
20. *Albert W. Atwood,* "Mergeritis."   102
21. *Ben Hecht,* "How's Chicago Now?"   106
22. *Dudley Glass,* "How's Atlanta Now?"   109

FARM, WORKSHOP, AND GHETTO   114

23. *Charles Moreau Harger,* "The Farmer and Three
    Dollar Wheat."   114
24. *Aaron Hardy Ulm,* "A Two Billion Dollar Cotton
    Crop."   118
25. *Samuel Gompers,* "Right Makes Might."   121
26. *Florence C. Thorne,* "Women and War Service."   124
27. *Ordway Tead,* "The New Place of Labor."   127
28. *Kingsley Moses,* "The Negro Comes North."   130
29. "Report to the Illinois State Council of Defense on
    the Race Riots at East St. Louis. . . ."   135
30. *John Richards,* "Some Experiences with Colored
    Soldiers."   140

INROADS ON CIVIL LIBERTIES   145

31. *Reinhold Niebuhr,* "The Failure of German-
    Americanism."   145
32. *Sarka B. Hrbkova,* " 'Bunk' in Americanization."   150
33. "Must We Go to Jail?"   155
34. "The Case of the Columbia Professors."   159
35. *John Lord O'Brien,* "Uncle Sam's Spy Policies."   163

PART III. PEACEMAKING, 1919–1920   169

TREATY DEBATE   171

36. William E. Borah, "Militarism in a League of
      Nations?"   171

37. Franklin H. Giddings, "Our Mythological History." 175

RADICALISM AND THE RED SCARE   179

38. Annie Pike Greenwood, "Letters from a Sage-Brush
      Farm."   179

39. Carleton H. Parker, "The I.W.W."   182

40. A. Mitchell Palmer, "The Case Against the " 'Reds.' " 185

RETURN TO "NORMALCY"   190

41. Harry Emerson Fosdick, "The Trenches and the
      Church at Home."   190

42. Jacob Gould Schurman, "New Ideals of Social
      Progress."   195

43. Charles Evans Hughes, "Our After-War Dangers." 198

44. Anthony Caminetti, "Need We Fear Immigration?" 203

Selected Bibliography   209

INTRODUCTION

World War I was an imposing watershed not only in the history of the United States but also in the pattern of world history. War has always been a mother of change, particularly in our time, aptly called a "century of total war" because international conflict now engages many more lives, extends over longer periods, and encompasses greater geographic areas than before. The deeper the struggle, the more catastrophic and unexpected the change associated with it. Such was certainly the case with World War I. The world of 1920 was vastly different than that of 1914. The bloodletting in France and elsewhere inaugurated a long season of plenary international violence that has still not run its course. Elsewhere I have called this global process "The Twentieth Century War," a term that indicates the profound interrelatedness of various wars since 1914.

For Americans World War I was both an end and a beginning. It was the last link in a long transition that spanned approximately the years 1840 to 1920 and transformed the United States into a modern urban-industrial society, one that was definitively differentiated from that older rural-agricultural society which had first flowered during the era of Jefferson and Jackson (1800–1835). The postwar decade of the 1920's, that "Era of Wonderful Nonsense," was the first distinctively "modern" period in the national experience. It was modern in the sense that for the first time historians of those years encounter a range of national attitudes, problems, reactions, and enterprises that bear a definite relationship to those of our own day. This claim cannot be made even for the decade immediately preceding the outbreak of the war (1904–1914).

Certainly the partisans of the Old America fought dramatic rearguard actions in the twenties, operating out of strongholds in the southland and the farther Middle West—that arc of states reaching from the Carolinas west to Texas and then north to the Dakotas. Chroniclers of the period cannot ignore a number of sensational controversies based on support for religious fundamentalism, notably over the teaching of biological evolution, prohibition of alcoholic drinks, and nativism, particularly as expressed in the activities of the Ku Klux Klan. The important thing about all these activities was that in each case the advocates of traditional viewpoints ultimately lost out. They were minorities composed mostly of those elements in American life who could not comprehend the changing conditions of life in the United States or who stood to suffer from change.

The events of the "Great War," as it is known in Europe, prepared the way for the triumph of the "modern" during the twenties. It brought to fruition a whole range of fundamental changes, underway since the middle years of the preceding century, changes that finally forced the passing of the old order. Historians have not fully grasped the importance of the period 1914–1920 for American social, cultural, and intellectual history because they have devoted most of their attention to the diplomatic and military history of the time. What actually went on *at home* during these years? How did the war abroad impinge on the lives of Americans who were not directly involved in stirring events abroad? The readings in this book illustrate the domestic experience of the American people during World War I. They are drawn from popular mass circulation magazines. The readings are "sources," part of the time itself, rather than secondary accounts prepared long after the events took place. They are organized in three groups. Part I considers the years of Neutrality (1914–1917) before the United States intervened in the European conflict. Part II deals with the period of Belligerency (1917–1918). Part III takes up the postwar reaction that occurred during the phase of Peacemaking (1919–1920).

NEUTRALITY, AUGUST 1914–APRIL 1917

The great European war that broke out in August of 1914 was almost completely unexpected in the United States. Americans were absorbed in the process of domestic reform called the "New Freedom" that President Woodrow Wilson was forcing through the Congress. They were hard put to grasp the reasons for the struggle and its extraordinary significance, but they were relatively quick to take sides. Sympathies gravitated largely to the "Allies" (Britain, France, Italy, Russia, and Japan) as against the "Central Powers" (Germany, Austria-Hungary, and Turkey), but few people in the United States favored American intervention. A strong consensus supported the policy of neutrality, pursued assiduously by the President and encouraged even by his most influential political opponents *(Reading 1)*. Only a few observers realized that the outbreak of war meant an end to a whole range of accepted thoughts and feelings that were deeply ingrained in American minds and hearts because they had served so well across the nineteenth century. According to the perspicacious Gertrude Stein, centuries begin slowly, and the twentieth was no exception. It did not reveal itself until August 1914, but a good many years passed before this reality became apparent to most people *(Reading 2)*.

The most evident consequence of the European struggle in the United States during its initial phase was its unsettling effect on the economy. A sharp recession took place in reaction to a vast dislocation of international exchange, trade, and commerce. Temporary difficulties soon passed, especially after the European belligerents began to place large war orders in the United States. Most of the orders came from the Allies because the British navy quickly established command of the surface sea and interdicted extensive commercial relations between neutral countries such as the United States and the Central Powers. Astute American businessmen were quick to profit from the war, and some of them quickly sensed the long-term changes that had been set in motion. Thomas W. Lamont, a partner in the famous investment banking firm of J. P. Morgan, drew attention to the economic consequences of the war, arguing that the United States could take economic advantage of the situation across the Atlantic and still contribute to the making of peace without sacrificing neutrality *(Reading 3)*.

War orders from Europe had immediate and imposing effects on communities in which such goods were produced. The small city of Bridgeport, Connecticut, where an important arms manufacturer was located, experienced rapid growth and prosperity but also certain attendant problems. Housing shortages and strains on municipal facilities were only the most obvious consequences of an interlude that was bound to cause profound long-run changes in the lives of the citizenry *(Reading 4)*. As the war years ran their course, many other cities underwent comparable experiences. Industrial expansion drew more and more people into the great urban centers of the nation, greatly accelerating the pattern of urbanization that had characterized the preceding half-century.

Despite the economic and social impact of the war, most Americans paid more attention to a burgeoning political debate about national defense. When it became obvious that the war would endure for some time and create challenges to American rights and interests, the nation engaged in an acrimonious debate between exponents of "preparedness" and those of "pacifism." Should the United States rapidly enlarge its military and naval forces in order to strengthen its defense against possible attack, or should the country avoid expenditures and policies that might conceivably involve it in the holocaust abroad? Those who favored preparedness held that it would help preserve neutrality. Opponents held that it would lead to belligerency.

In 1915 and 1916 the term "pacifist" encompassed nearly everyone who opposed a greatly augmented national defense. Women were among the earliest and most conspicuous leaders of the antiwar and eventually the antipreparedness faction. Of this group none was more influential than Jane Addams, the famous social worker from Hull House in Chicago. She quickly linked the cause of peace with that of women's rights, thus attracting to the peace movement the rank-and-file supporters of some of the most enthusiastic crusades of the time, particularly those in behalf of national prohibition and votes for women

(Reading 5). Another conspicious contingent of pacifists came from American churches. Religious publicists for nonviolence expressed their views forcefully in the public print, often citing the example of Jesus Christ to buttress their opinions *(Reading 6).* Other opponents of preparedness were supporters of the "Progressive Movement" for social and economic justice that had absorbed the country for a decade and more. Spokesmen for this large element believed that militarization would inhibit humanizing reform both at home and in the world. They had no doubt that war was incompatible with human progress *(Reading 7).*

Advocates of preparedness such as Theodore Roosevelt and General Leonard Wood were convinced that military and naval strength was an essential prerequisite for any influential role in international politics. Often hopeful of stimulating more national organization and discipline, they maintained that revolutionized conditions at home and abroad required a novel national attitude toward defense *(Reading 8).* The presidential election of 1916 was in some ways a referendum on preparedness. President Wilson, at least a near-pacifist, supported some limited defense measures to draw the teeth of his critics while making enormous political capital out of the slogan "He kept us out of war." Not surprisingly, most supporters of preparedness favored the unsuccessful Republican candidate, Charles Evans Hughes. The controversy over preparedness extended into many areas of public concern; for example, rival educators broadly debated the propriety of introducing military training into schools and colleges *(Reading 9, 10).* This argument was symptomatic of changing concerns forced on a reluctant people by the war in Europe.

As it happened, event rather than rhetoric ultimately determined the outcome of the domestic political argument. Early in 1917 the leaders of Germany decided that the Central Powers could force a favorable decision in the war by means of a single quick stroke—unrestricted submarine assault on neutral commerce trading across the high seas to the Allied nations. Undersea warfare, of course, would chiefly affect the United States, by far the most important of the neutral shippers. Earlier, in connection with crises caused when German submarines sank the *Lusitania* (1915) and the *Sussex* (1916), President Wilson refused to condone unrestricted submarine warfare, more or less committing himself to war if Germany resumed the practice. On the other hand, for two long and frustrating years he sought energetically to bring about a negotiated peace, one he ultimately called "peace without victory." Neither side was prepared to accept Wilsonian mediation because each persisted in the view that it could eventually achieve a decisive victory. The German undersea initiative of January 1917 forced an end to mediation efforts. Public opinion across America rapidly shifted to support of intervention in the European war, a process reinforced by "overt acts" on the part of Germany *(Reading 11).*

The relatively rapid transition from neutral to belligerent attitudes necessitated an appealing rationalization, and the nation found one in short order. The war would be fought not for selfish national gain but for the universal goals of freedom and democracy. This justification appealed strongly to President Wilson himself, who utilized it in his war message of April 2, 1917, but others anticipated his argument, even conservative and anti-Wilsonian organs such as the *North American Review (Reading 12).* The "war to end all wars" would "make the world safe for democracy." Despite his passionate hatred of war, the President choose belligerency because he decided that only by fighting could the United States exert a dominating influence on the ultimate peace settlement. Armed intervention was a means to the supreme end of a just and lasting peace. When Congress voted its war resolution on April 6, 1917, the United States definitively abandoned a century and more of fixed diplomatic tradition—the policy of "isolation." If the intervention had no parallel in American foreign relations, it also exerted unprecedented influence on life at home.

President Wilson carefully delayed his decision for war until it was broadly acceptable to the great majority of the American people, but significant minorities refused to grant either the expediency or the necessity of war. Among the dissenters were conscientious objectors to war on religious grounds. One young objector, Norman Thomas, who later became the leader of the

American socialists, summarized the views of this group effectively (*Reading 13*). Many intellectuals who had opposed preparedness lent support to the war, a tendency that drew mordant criticism from one of the most intriguing writers of the period, Randolph Bourne, who refused to adopt the optimistic view that the experience of war could be turned to good account (*Reading 14*). Nay-sayers like Bourne were quite rare. Such voices were lost in the clamor of those who began immediately to organize the human and material resources of the nation for war. Speed was essential; Germany had unleashed her submarines in the belief that the war would be won before the Americans could bring their power to bear.

BELLIGERENCY, APRIL 1917–NOVEMBER 1918

The first wartime task was "mobilization"—gearing up the nation for a vast military and naval effort. Precedent for such activity was lacking, and the nation was woefully unready for combat. A critical aspect of the enterprise was the mobilization of hearts and minds. Accordingly, propagandists quickly produced a spate of heated articles to stimulate hatred of the enemy and support for the war effort. Louise Maunsell Field's "Sentimentalizing Over the Hun" is a good example of this literature. In comparing the German people with ancient barbarians, it indirectly attacked President Wilson's attempt to assign war guilt to irresponsible leaders rather than the whole German people (*Reading 15*). To coordinate the propaganda effort Wilson placed the energetic journalist George Creel at the head of a Committee on Public Information. One of Creel's projects was the organization of a huge oratorical effort, the "Four Minute Men," an army of some 75,000 speakers prepared to boost the war with brief speeches at motion picture theaters, conventions, and other public gatherings. The government enlisted the ingenuity of painters to produce attractive billboards and posters publicizing wartime appeals and programs. No radio or television existed at the time; graphic art played an important role in an effective "sell" (*Reading 16*). By such devices modern warfare reached into every life. Even children were not exempt. Florence Woolston's sensitive report in the *New Republic* on "Billy and the World War" indicates the ways in which the activities of the Committee on Public Information caught up little boys and girls *(Reading 17)*.

The central aspect of mobilization, of course, was the organization of the economy for war production. Without this endeavor the War and Navy Departments could not have prepared fighting units for the combat zones or provisioned the armies and navies of the Allies in the interim between the American intervention and the arrival of its forces at the fighting fronts. The exigencies of mobilization, particularly the need for rapid and thorough execution, required a degree of government intervention in the private enterprise economy that would have been inconceivable in any other context than the most extreme national emergency. In a trice the nation accepted controls that would never have occurred in the wildest dreams of the most advanced Progressive advocates of government regulation. Various government agencies, such as the Council on National Defense and the War Industries Board, were established to provide central direction and coordination. The task proved intensely difficult. There was great confusion and delay, but it was accomplished well enough to ensure a decisive economic and military reinforcement of the beleaguered Allies *(Reading 18)*. No emergency war agency was more energetic than the United States Food Administration, headed by Herbert C. Hoover, which attempted to provide high levels of agricultural production, rational patterns of distribution, and appropriate prices *(Reading 19)*.

The experience of mobilization influenced the future. It served as model for a later generation of leaders who, in 1933, confronted another national emergency, the Great Depression, when extensive government intervention and control of the economy again became necessary. Some of the most influential builders of the early New Deal, including President Franklin D. Roosevelt himself, who was Assistant Secretary of the Navy during 1917-1918, were veterans of wartime Washington. Another consequence of the mobilization, unexpected and ironic, was its tendency to encourage marked industrial concentration or "mergeritis," only recently a prime bugaboo of many Progressive reformers who considered "trustbusting" next to Godliness *(Reading 20)*.

The imperative requirement of national unity lessened sectional strife during the war, but distinctive regional traditions and attitudes helped the people to weather the conflict. In Chicago and Atlanta, for example, the citizenry reacted in terms of distinctions between the Middle West and the South, but in both places there was a common objective—to contribute all that was possible to victory *(Readings 21, 22)*.

The war years deeply affected American agriculture. Greatly expanded markets for agricultural products caused skyrocketing output and prices, but inflation and increased costs of production often offset much of the profit accruing to farmers. The Food Administration and other government agencies encouraged maximum production and price stability, obviously competitive objectives. Farmers generally had good years during the war emergency, but a widespread agricultural recession began as early as 1921 because of unwise wartime investment and expansion as well as postwar circumstances. For many farmers government controls on prices and other aspects of government intervention in the economy were a mixed blessing. They wanted to do all in their power to support the war effort. They responded avidly to the slogan "Food will win the war," but they also aspired to a good profit *(Readings 23, 24)*.

The mobilization of 1917–1918 had truly important consequences for industrial workers. The war meant gains in terms of hours, wages, and working conditions for the armed services. Labor leaders, including the venerable president of the American Federation of Labor, Samuel Gompers, were quick to argue that a war to make the world safe for democracy should not provide cover for unfair labor practices at home *(Reading 25)*. Proponents of equal rights for women used the opportunity presented by the war, when women moved into the factories in great numbers, to argue the case that equal work should receive equal compensation. Gains made by women at this time foreshadowed the "emancipation" of the twenties *(Reading 26)*.

Some labor leaders played important roles in government, and it seemed to some observers that the prestige and power accruing to labor would ensure progress toward industrial democracy during the immediate postwar years. As it happened, these wartime expectations were not completely fulfilled, but the activities of working men and women during the mobilization represented an important step forward in the organization of American labor and its acceptance as a legitimate interest group on the national scene *(Reading 27)*.

The American Negro community experienced a great upheaval during World War I. The remarkable expansion of American industry and the consequent demand for labor inspired a great migration of southern Negroes to the booming industrial cities of the North. Nothing like it had ever occurred before *(Reading 28)*. For some who took part, the change meant nothing less than emancipation, but there were some tragic consequences as well. Urban life was strange and often debilitating for Negroes who had lived in the rural South. Moreover, in some congested cities serious racial disturbances took place. None was more excruciating than the riot in East St. Louis, Illinois, in June 1917, but there were all too many others elsewhere, a clear indication that racial tension was a national phenomenon *(Reading 29)*. Many Negroes served in the armed forces, although little effective integration took place in the army and navy. The service of Negro soldiers in France excited some interest and sympathy, but the power of ingrained racial stereotypes and prejudices was too considerable to be dispensed with in one fell swoop, even in the crucible of war *(Reading 30)*. Historians of today's conflicts over civil rights must return to the past at least as far as World War I to discern the origins of recent urban unrest, a striking example of the continuity of "modern" America since that time.

The United States fought during World War I in the name of freedom, but antilibertarian practices emerged within the "temple of freedom" itself. The most widespread challenge to personal liberties was the prejudicial and discriminatory treatment of German-Americans. Allegations of treason appeared on every hand, but only a few cases of disloyalty were actually documented, proof that the wish was father to the thought *(Reading 31)*. The onset of belligerency stimulated various "Americanization" crusades, derivative in part from anti-immigration campaigns that had begun before the war. These movements stressed the eradication of foreign loyalties and customs among nationality groups already in the country as well as restraints on future immigration. The "Americanization" movements ran counter to the much-praised tradition of cultural pluralism, and too often they were aimed at individuals and groups who by no stretch of the imagination could be suspected of disloyalty *(Reading 32)*.

When conformity pressures are great, inroads on freedom of thought and expression are likely to occur. Some notable examples of this phenomenon apply to the war years. The federal government placed rather severe controls on the press, measures to which many newspapers and magazines responded indignantly, arguing that the legislation violated constitutional rights *(Reading 33)*. When voices of dissent rose in the academic community, nervous administrators reacted improperly in some cases, notably at Columbia University *(Reading 34)*. State and local branches of the Council of National Defense often condoned repressive measures that stifled unpopular causes and minority opinions. On the other hand, the vitality of civil liberty became apparent when its defenders rose on all sides to protest such activities. The United States experienced less repression than any of the other leading belligerents; the Department of Justice showed considerable awareness of the dangers of excess during the war *(Reading 35)*. The American Civil Liberties Union was founded during this time specifically to preserve those American rights and freedoms challenged at home during the war to make the world safe for democracy.

PEACEMAKING, NOVEMBER 1918–1920

The Central Powers found themselves forced to surrender abjectly only nineteen months after the United States entered the war. Of course, Europe had fought for thirty-one desperate months before the American intervention. The speed of victory stemmed in large part from the impact of the American reinforcement, which materialized rapidly enough to provide the necessary margin. Ironically, many wartime projects never came to fruition because the conflict came to an abrupt end much sooner than had been anticipated, even by the rosiest optimists. By November 1918 the victors and vanquished of Europe were completely exhausted, but the United States had still to reach the zenith of its power. For this reason President Wilson was in good position to shape the outcome of the postwar peace negotiations, exactly the object that had led to his decision for war. Soon after the armistice of November 11, 1918, Wilson went to Europe to negotiate for the United States at the Paris Peace Conference. There he was able to force a settlement that approximated the program for the postwar world laid out initially during 1918 in the famous Fourteen Points and associated pronouncements. The Treaty of Versailles was not without notable imperfections, but it was undeniably "Wilsonian" in nature, providing as it did for a re-established European balance and an international collective security organization. Critics of the settlement often overemphasize its failings and ignore its many virtues.

President Wilson had enjoyed great popularity during 1917–1918 both at home and abroad because he made himself the symbol of the worldwide yearning for an end to the war and a just and lasting peace, but his unparalleled international prestige did not survive a pervasive postwar reaction. As his intentions became apparent in Paris, supporters in other nations who experienced real or imagined losses fell away from him. A comparable process occurred at home. War raises the people to the highest pitch of energy and sacrifice. When war ends, a letdown is almost inevitable. Although the United States had been at war for a relatively brief period and had exerted itself far less than the other great powers, the domestic reaction came rapidly and intensely. The experience of international warfare was novel and unsettling for Americans. Many wondered whether unwise precedent had been established, asking themselves whether national security really required the intervention. The

war had set in motion forces that seriously undermined established life styles and patterns. In addition to these more general
sources of tension, a number of specific influences combined to
undermine support for the President and his peace treaty. Certain ethnic groups whose homelands had been rebuffed in Paris
such as the Italian-Americans and Irish-Americans became rabid
antagonists of ratification. Some leaders of the Republican Party
believed that acceptance of the Treaty of Versailles would guar-
antee victory for the Democratic Party in the elections of 1920.
Many liberals who earlier had supported Wilson became wary
because of flaws in the treaty and the belief that international
entanglements might inhibit reform at home. Political con-
servatives feared that membership in the League of Nations
might require the nation to surrender critical aspects of its
sovereignty.

Certainly President Wilson's vision of the future imposed on
the American people truly important changes in national policy—
the burdens of power. The thought of those future responsibilities often excited great anxiety, especially given extraordinary
changes already wrought by the recent wartime experience.
Nothing was more influential in shaping attitudes than the
onset of the Bolshevik Revolution in Russia with its explicit
rejection of nearly all the trappings of liberal bourgeois democracy. Many people believed that Bolshevism might sweep
across the entire world to engulf even the United States in the
wake of wartime devastation. It was possible to infer some kind
of insidious connection between the liberal reforms of Wilson
and the revolutionary principles of Lenin. Of course, in reality
Wilson's program directly challenged the radicalism of the
Bolsheviks as well as the reactionary outlook of Europe's *ancien
régime*.

Opponents of the treaty settlement argued persuasively that
the changes urged by Wilson were either unnecessary or dangerous. The most extreme critics held that they were subversive
of American ideals and traditions. The debate over ratification
was in one dimension a controversy over the nature of the American past and the American future. Senator William E. Borah,
a progressive Republican from Idaho and one of the most ener-

getic opponents of ratification, reiterated conventional views of American history and American destiny that seemed inaccurate and even dangerous to those such as the historian Franklin Giddings who believed that the times required fundamental changes in national thought and practice *(Readings 36, 37)*.

No national development contributed more to the abandonment of wartime reformism than the "Great Red Scare" of 1919–1920. It was a response to the belief, clearly unfounded, that radicals were about to overthrow the established order. The supposed growth of radical political activity in the United States in the wake of victory was an extension of the wartime penchant for discerning enemy spies behind every bush. To be sure, in the Dakotas and adjacent states a new organization had been founded to defend the interests of farmers, one that was clearly within the tradition that had produced the Grange, the Alliances, and finally the Populist movement at the end of the preceding century. The Non-Partisan League put forward a comprehensive program of agrarian reform which was easily misrepresented by its opponents as communism in disguise *(Reading 38)*. The activities of a truly radical labor organization, the International Workers of the World, also lent spurious legitimacy to the case of those who feared revolution within. Scholars who investigated the I.W.W. revealed its true nature *(Reading 39)*. Even the activities of the American Socialist Party, whose leader, Eugene V. Debs, had been imprisoned for antiwar activity, seemed to some to herald massive dangers. All this stimulated an extensive antisubversive campaign against Americans who supposedly had become implicated in revolutionary plots, a "righteous crusade" directed by the Attorney General of the United States, A. Mitchell Palmer. He authorized a large number of raids and arrests, some of which led to deportations, and in the process flouted much of the Bill of Rights *(Reading 40)*. The Red Scare did not endure for long; it dissipated rapidly after Palmer's excesses became obvious and his frightening allegations were proved to be unfounded.

The Red Scare has come to symbolize the unwillingness of the American people to accept the lessons of World War I. Certainly the skillful politics of a small group of senators and their supporters was a prime reason for the failure of the United States to ratify the Treaty of Versailles. On the other hand, acceptance of its obligations entailed great departures from tradition, the shouldering of international responsibilities undreamed of in the past that would have remarkable effects on life at home. The Red Scare fed on nameless fears stirred by the scarifying prospect of future change as well as on the jarring experience of the war just past. Wilson had been able to force acceptance of his domestic reforms, but his more fundamental projects for international reform proved too much to swallow.

Prophets of the need to accept change were not lacking in the immediate postwar years. A man who later became one of the most renowned Protestant ministers in the country, Harry Emerson Fosdick, called on the nation's churchpeople to recognize the challenge presented by returning soldiers. As it happened, Fosdick's fellow citizens largely ignored his highminded arguments *(Reading 41)*. Continuing attempts to develop support for at least a modicum of Wilsonian internationalism fell by the wayside in 1920 *(Reading 42)*.

In November 1920 Senator Warren G. Harding of Ohio won a landslide victory in the presidential election; the electorate thoroughly repudiated the candidates of the Democratic Party who stood uncertainly on the domestic and international record of Woodrow Wilson. The results made definite and certain what had been increasingly obvious for many months—that the country wished to return to what Harding called "normalcy." Americans sought relief from the extraordinary pressures and responsibilities that they had endured during the emergency. Even the most responsible Republicans such as Charles Evans Hughes took advantage of the national desire for respite in presenting the case against Wilson and all his works *(Reading 43.)* The urge to "normalcy" was a natural concomitant of that fear of change which undergirded the Red Scare. Historians discern in the notable xenophobia of the wartime years an initial indication of the mood that developed into an irresistible floodtide almost as soon as the fighting stopped in Europe. Even the Wilsonians themselves often succumbed to this tendency during the last year and a half of the stricken leader's second term. Many policies that became fully established during the twenties had their origins in the activities of discredited Democrats during 1919 and 1920; for example, comments on the prospects for postwar immigration from Europe by the Commissioner of Immigration, Anthony Caminetti, reveal some of the anti-immigration attitudes that became fully apparent during the Harding Administration *(Reading 44)*.

The apparent virtues of the "business civilization" that grew up during the twenties seemed to confirm the wisdom of those who called for "normalcy." A "success-exhaustion syndrome" tormented the body politic. After all, the war had been won as a direct result of American intervention. The successful campaign in Europe had certainly preserved and in fact greatly enhanced the security of the Republic. The effort had been exhausting. Hadn't enough been accomplished? The result, supposedly, was the reaction of the twenties.

As it happened, however, nothing like a return to the prewar *status quo* was possible. The war had accelerated or set in motion all manner of social, economic, cultural, and intellectual change. The readings in this book illustrate many of them. The victory of the "modern" was all but complete even before the beginning of the Roaring Twenties. Even abroad the United States pursued foreign policies that departed most significantly from the prewar pattern. The supposed repudiation of Wilson and all his works proclaimed by the priesthood of the "New Era" obscured what had come about within America the Beautiful during the war, even as it disguised innovations in foreign policy.

In one of the most remarkable American novels of the twenties, F. Scott Fitzgerald's *The Great Gatsby*, one finds the obituary of the Old America. Jay Gatsby was done to death because he persisted in a noble but superannuated faith in the traditions of the American past. Jay dreamed a simple and powerful version of the American Dream. He failed to consider the overwhelming evidence around him that the time for living as he sought to live was gone. Jay pursued Daisy Buchanan, his meretricious dream made flesh, but she was in fact unworthy of Gatsby, careless, with her voice that sounded like money. In chronicling the tragedy of Gatsby, Fitzgerald educated his generation to the necessity of accepting the dangers and opportunities of "modernity." This novel could not have been written before 1914. World War I vastly altered the course of world history. An aspect of that global phenomenon was its effect on American lives. The events of 1914–1920 prepared the way not only for the Era of Wonderful Nonsense but for the rest of the century as well.

PART ONE

Neutrality, 1914–1917

The United States must be neutral in fact as well as in name during these days that are to try men's souls. We must be impartial in thought as well as action, must put a curb on our sentiments as well as upon every transaction that might be construed as a preference of one party to the struggle before another. PRESIDENT WOODROW WILSON, AUGUST 1914.

INITIAL SHOCK

1   *William Howard Taft*
A Message to the People of the United States

The reaction of a former Republican President (1909–1913) *to the sudden onset of World War I accurately reflected the general shock and confusion of the American people in August, 1914. Taft's statement also mirrored the widespread desire to establish a firm neutrality. Ironically, the Republican leader sounded a theme that President Woodrow Wilson, a Democrat, later made his own — the hope that the great struggle would be a war to end all wars.*

As I write, Germany is reported to have declared war against Russia and France, and the participation of England on the one side and of Italy on the other seems imminent. Nothing like it has occurred since the great Napoleonic wars, and with modern armaments and larger populations nothing has occurred like it since the world began.

It is a cataclysm. It is a retograde step in Christian civilization. It will be difficult to keep the various countries of the Balkans out of the war, and Greece and Turkey may take part in it. All Europe is to be a battleground. It is reported that the neutrality of Holland has already been ignored and Belgium offers such opportunities in the campaigns certain to follow that

SOURCE. William Howard Taft, "A Message to the People of the United States," *Independent* (1914), **79**:198–199.

her territory, too, will be the scene of struggle.

Private property and commercial shipping under an enemy's flag are subject to capture and appropriation by prize proceedings and with the formidable navies of England, France, Germany, Russia and Italy active the great carrying trade of the world will be in large part suspended or destroyed or will be burdened with such heavy insurance as greatly to curtail it.

The commerce of the world makes much for the prosperity of the countries with whom it is conducted and its interruption means great inconvenience and economic suffering among all people, whether at peace or war. The capital which the European people have invested by the billions in the United States, Canada, Australia, South Africa and in the Orient must perforce be withdrawn to fill the war chests of the nations engaged in a death grapple, and the enterprises which that capital made possible are likely to be greatly crippled while the hope of any further expansion must be definitely given up.

This general European war will give a feverish activity in a number of branches of our industry, but on the whole we shall suffer with the rest of the world, except that we shall not be destroying or blowing up our existing wealth or sacrificing the lives of our best young men and youth.

It is hard to prophesy the scope of a war like this because history offers no precedent. It is impossible to foresee the limits of a war of any proportions when confined only to two countries. In our own small Spanish war we began it to free Cuba and when the war closed we found ourselves ten thousand miles away with the Philippines on our hands.

The immense waste of life and treasure in a modern war makes the loss to the conqueror only less, if indeed it be less, than the loss to the conquered.

With a high patriotic spirit, people enter upon war with confidence and with the thought of martial glory and success. The sacrifices they have to make, the suffering they have to undergo are generally such that if victory does not rest upon their banners they seek a scapegoat for that which they themselves have brought on in the head of the state, and the king or emperor who begins a war or allows one to begin puts at stake not only the prestige of his nation but also the stability and integrity of his dynasty.

In such a war as this, therefore, with the universal tendency to popular control in every country, the strain and defeat in war may lead to a state of political flux in those countries which shall suffer defeat, with all the attendant difficulties and disorder that a change of government involves.

While we can be sure that such a war as this, taking it by and large, will be a burden upon the United States and is a great misfortune, looked at solely from the standpoint of the United States, we have every reason to be happy that we are able to preserve strict neutrality in respect to it. Within our hospitable boundaries we have living prosperous and contended emigrants in large numbers from all the countries who are to take part in the war and the sympathies of these people will of course be with their respective native lands. Were there no other reason this circumstance would tend to keep us free from an entanglement.

We may sincerely hope that Japan will not be involved. She will not be unless the war is carried on to the far Orient, to India or to China. Germany has but a small settlement in the Orient, while France and Russia and England would be allies in this war and it would seem quite unlikely that there would arise any obligation under the English-Japanese alliance for Japan to assist England.

Of the great powers of the world, therefore, the only ones left out are likely to be the United States and Japan, and perhaps only the United States, by reason of the alliance between Japan and England. Japan, if she keeps out of the war, will occupy the same advantageous position, which will be ours, of complete neutrality, of an actually judicial attitude, and therefore, of having an opportunity at some time, we may hope, to mediate between the powers and to help to mitigate this disaster to mankind.

At the time when so many friends of peace have thought that we were making real progress toward the abolition of war this sudden outbreak of the greatest war in history is most discouraging. The future looks dark indeed, but we should not despair.

"God moves in a mysterious way His wonders to perform." Now that the war is a settled fact, we must hope that some good may come from this dreadful scourge. The armaments of Europe had been growing heavier and heavier, bankruptcy has stared many of the nations in the face, conflict between races had begun to develop.

War seemed likely at some stage and the question which each country had to answer for itself was at what time the situation would be most favorable for its success. The immediate participants have decided that the time has come and through their international alliance all Europe is involved.

There has been no real test of the heavy armament on land or water as developed by modern invention and this contest is to show what has been well spent for war purposes and what has been wasted. It is by no means certain that waste will not exceed in cost that which was spent to effective purpose.

One thing I think we can reasonably count on is that with the prostration of industry, with the blows of prosperity, with the state of flux that is likely to follow this titanic struggle, there will be every opportunity for common sense to resume its sway; and after the horrible expenditure of the blood of the best and the savings of the rich and the poor, the opportunity and the motive for a reduction of armament and the taking away of a temptation to further war will be greatly enhanced.

It is an awful remedy, but in the end it may be worth what it costs, if it makes this the last great war. The influence of America can be thrown most effectively for peace when peace is possible and for minimum armaments when disaster and exhaustion shall make the contending peoples and their rulers see things as they are.

2 Mental Unpreparedness

This editorial from a leading liberal journal draws attention to the intellectual misapprehensions that prevented Americans from recognizing the true direction of world politics. The themes of this statement anticipated many of the most significant strains in later twentieth-century American thought, including a broad-ranging critique of simplistic nineteenth-century theories of natural and inevitable progress.

To a younger generation brought up with a humanitarian and evolutionist philosophy the war has been a shock that has dislodged all the old ideals. If the conflict had been over speedily, we might have dismissed it as a momentary aberration of our civilized world. The Balkan Wars we could view calmly because they were too palpably contests between half-formed nations to shake our faith in the bettering Europe. But the war has not been speedy. And now after a year what was a shock in which the very universe seemed to reel has become almost the normal background of European affairs. We no longer ask how it can all be got back to its original state, but what the outcome will do to our world, while a year ago we could not have been fairly dragooned into accepting the fact that it is exactly in the sort of world where such things happen that we live and may live for years to come.

That background of ours which was shattered by the iron touch of *Weltkrieg* was primarily one of social evolution. We studied the customs and movements of the peoples, the economic structure of society, rather than the life of camps and courts, the intrigues of rulers, and the bargainings and warfares of states. The "new history" told us how the peoples lived and worked, how they were conditioned by geographical environ-

SOURCE. "Mental Unpreparedness," *New Republic* (September 11, 1915), 143–144.

ment. History became the clue to that understanding of society to which intellectual enthusiasm in these latter days has shifted itself.

The nineteenth century, which gave us the immediate setting for today, was sketched for us in wholly beneficent lines as an irresistible progress. The colossus of the industrial revolution almost smothered that French Revolution for which the orthodox historians had been the parting of the ways. The inventors loomed larger than the statesmen. We traced the clamors for political democracy to the root of industrial progress and found in the transformation of the means of production and communication the clue to that contemporary history which we studied with so much eagerness. Indeed, in the colleges it was exactly this modern time and the forces that had produced it that we most heavily emphasized. We studied comparative government, we knew the outlines of the labor movement and the extension of the suffrage in the various countries. We studied contemporary philosophers, Bergson, Nietzsche, the pragmatists. Current foreign literature made its way into the college course. It was to the modern world that that part of young America which has fallen under intellectual influences during the past ten years has chiefly devoted itself.

And yet, though no generation ever studied so closely its own environment, the war caught us almost staggeringly unprepared. It was not that our material was incorrect or our interest vain. It was rather that all our interpretations had led us to expect a different denouement to the drama. At the clinch we were to find that the forces which we had seen as the motivating ones were weaker than others more traditional, which had dropped to a subordinate place in our minds. Our cosmopolitanism had made us forget that the European states represented very tight and integrated cultures, with very diverse histories, group-wills, philosophies. We had inadvertantly washed the colors out of our maps and left only geographical boundary lines between the peoples, whom we tended to think of as psychically like ourselves. In putting our attention on "movements," we had neglected the richly woven fabrics of the diverse "Kulturs." We persistently thought of democracy, universal suffrage, equal rights, social legislation as benevolent diseases which were spreading through one after another of the nations of Europe. We made these movements into things-in-themselves, and they, rather than the entire culture situation, became the realities for us. Our young historians could speak of "the ever-recurring and increasingly successful movements throughout Europe for the extension of the suffrage, and the removal of legal disabilities in society," as if national differences were only differences of democratic altitude, and the same advancing wave would slowly and automatically rise above them all.

The Russian revolution, the Young Turks, Portugal, China marked for us the ascent of the waters. Where we might have seen the Russians endeavoring to transcend the tepid constitutionalism of the western world in the interests of a truly social state on occupational lines, where we might have seen the political resurrection of the Ottoman as the fruit of German intrigue, where we might have predicted the dictatorship of Yuan-Shi-Kai, here we preferred only to see the nations strung along a straight line of democratic progress and straining all in the same direction. We scarcely saw that we were naively postulating an Anglo-Saxon standard as the goal for all.

After democracy we saw the coming of social control. When the peoples should have caught the benevolent disease of democracy, we saw them behaving in the interests of deliberate social betterment. "The people of each affected state," says a recent book, "thought of using their democratic representative mastery over government as a means to undertake industrial regulation and general social control." And we studied the forms of social politics in the different countries, scarcely stopping to analyze the motivations which made laws in Baden mean something wholly different from the same laws in France. Always the emphasis was on the quality—the democracy, the representative mastery, the social politics—instead of on the country as a whole, with its attitudes and aspirations, its peculiar ways of interpreting itself, the interplay of its classes.

The interpretation of Europe in terms of democratic quality was immensely reinforced by international socialism. Here, at least, was a common force, an international political party. And the discovery that there were socialisms taking the color of the different cultures, rather than Socialism, was perhaps the hardest challenge which our old background received from the war. Even nationality we saw in innocent terms, unsaturated with the menace of today. The integration of Germany and Italy in the nineteenth century came to our minds as noble attainments, not beginnings. National aspirations were veiled to us by the peace movement and the half-truths of Norman-Angellism. We saw only the internationalizing forces, which were in truth there. The peace movement seemed another of those benevolent diseases which should speedily bless mankind. To hasten its work, an American had built an inoculating station at The Hague. Peace took the guise of the mere prevention of war. The map became a symbol of fixity of status. All the "problems of power," the conflict of interests, we deprecated as unreal. Such talk was the professional bias of decaying military caste, which we saw everywhere as on the defensive. The real powers were the industrial and democratic elements. The language in which international affairs were discussed we dismissed as diplomatic jargon. Even when we saw the wagon trains and regiments in European streets we could not take them seriously. We saw them only as a costly form of insurance. An armed peace, but essentially a *peace!* Increased armaments served to insure against calamity.

Everything conspired them to make our background of contemporary Europe that most perilous of things—a field where a benevolent destiny was working itself out unaided. And nothing is more blinding than belief in a progress which is not conditioned by deliberate human intelligence. For to recognize the balking of the benevolent destiny seems too flagrantly like surrendering our whole host of ideals. If we have learned anything from a year of war, it is that we shall have to face a world very different from that with which our current imaginations have grown up. Are we to refuse to face it and call our refusal idealism? Are we to balk at finding nationalism to be, instead of a finished ideal, an infinitely dynamic urge, at finding potent ideals of valor and collectivism which bear solidly against the direction in which we saw civilization to be moving? Are we to content ourselves with anger and with a mere reiteration of our old ideals? Shall we still talk of "immutable principles" and petrify our desires? Shall we continue to make English conceptions of democracy and progress the measuring-rod for the nations? Shall we say, "Though it slay me, yet will I still trust in the nineteenth century?"

These are hard questions. Their very expression will seem to many to be a shameful surrender. Yet if we stand indomitably by our idealistic guns, shall we not perhaps put ourselves in the tragic position of being able to face the truth only by losing our ideals. To be immutable is really to be false to our whole American pragmatic philosophy. The war has been the first real test of that attitude. We are at the parting of the intellectual ways. We can put our ideals behind us and turn and worship them, or we can put them ahead of us and struggle towards them. It is an issue between an old immutable idealism and a new experimental idealism. We can reiterate or we can explore. To screw our ideals a notch higher, to live in a new century, does not mean spiritual defeat. We do not need to surrender. But we emphatically need to understand.

While the world is breathless, we can try resolutely to reconstruct our shattered background, find out what kind of a world we live in. We should make the time one of education and not of prophecy or objurgation or bewailing. No one knows what will come. Certainly merely getting the war over will not bring back the old ideals. If we desire that new world where all can live, we must first thoroughly understand how all want to live. Our education can be in the way of learning what each nation thinks it is doing and in comparing its pretensions with the good life which it has been able to build for itself, as a society and as a family of individuals. New ideas can work out only from such a vantage ground of fact. The war gives us the incomparable opportunity of laying that foundation of stern realism of which to build our new ideals. And those new ideals must come, not in terms of metaphysical qualities as before, but in terms of the concretely envisaged good life, built on science, illumined with art, happy with intelligence and equality. But only by understanding what Europe is now shall we be able to understand the Europe that the war will leave and the Europe that it may become. Only by becoming acquainted with the peoples, their wills, their philosophies, their "Kulturs," shall we save ourselves from being caught by some new crisis intellectually unprepared.

3   *Thomas W. Lamont*
Financial Illusions of the War

The author, a partner in the House of Morgan, astutely analyzes the economic opportunities of the war as well as the dangers it posed for the American people. Lamont punctures a series of false theories in the process. An "establishment" figure, the investment banker frequently responded to calls from Washington for sage counsel.

The war has been breaking down principles, overturning axioms, shattering theories, in every direction. We have seen this statement overwhelmingly proved in military, in naval affairs. No less is it true in finance. In the school of finance, as well as that of the army and navy, there were certain tenets that men had long clung to which have proved to be great illusions.

To begin with, there was the favorite theory that the great international bankers could prevent war. . . . When, however, the storm clouds of the present war were gathering, the opinion of the great groups of bankers counted apparently for nothing. Their judgment counted enormously in the steps that were taken by the different governments to maintain financial equilibrium, but on the main question of war or peace they were not even

SOURCE. Thomas W. Lamont, "Financial Illusions of the War," *Harper's Magazine* (1916), 133:206–212. Copyright © 1916 by *Harper's Magazine*, Inc. Reprinted from the July 1916 issue of *Harper's Magazine* by permission of the publisher.

consulted. And so, on August 1, 1914, this interesting theory was disposed of promptly, and perhaps for all time.

The explanation is not far to seek: no one of the governments involved stopped to say: "Wait a bit. Before I spend the money let me first find out whether I can raise it." On the contrary, to these governments, all plunging headlong down the steep, the money cost was the least thing to think of—and quite properly, too, if one compare with it the matter of human lives, liberty, and national honor!

Another financial theory that has had to be discarded is that the cost of a world war, such as this, was bound to be so stupendous as to enforce an early peace. Even the richest nations would not be able (the theory ran) to stand the pace. But here we have had almost two years of war, and as yet there seems to be no indication of the war ending on account of financial exhaustion. . . .

But when the present war broke out the *per diem* cost of $5,000,000, as estimated by the financial philosophers, had to be altered in the case of Great Britain to $10,000,000. And the Prime Minister and the Chancellor of the Exchequer warned the British people that such a slow pace could not last. They were quite right. Each month, by leaps and bounds, the expenditure increased; and Mr. Asquith, in his last statement, confessed to $25,000,000 per day as the outgo. And the total daily expenditure of the belligerents is now estimated at over $100,000,000. . . .

There is still a third financial tradition that has had to be abandoned. This is the one that international trade and exchange, soundly built up for a series of generations, was so firmly established that nothing could wreck it. Another great illusion! For when the war came our exchanges broke down overnight. The whole structure, whereby the cattlemen in Argentine, the farmer in Dakota, the diamond-miner in Africa, the silk merchant in China, could get their pay or could settle their bills, as the case might be, without serious loss in exchange, came toppling down like a house of cards. Coincident with, and following, this downfall were to be seen all the phenomena of a world topsy-turvy. All precedent, all traditions, went by the board. As Frederick Scott Oliver says, in his admirable *Ordeal by Battle,* there is no further use in declaring a thing unthinkable when we have only to look about us and see that the unthinkable has become true. . . .

With these fond illusions lying fresh-shattered just behind them, economists, nothing daunted, are now laying down fresh theories. One favorite and rashly expressed belief is that all the warring nations, big as well as little, are about to plunge over the brink into repudiation and bankruptcy. The propagandists of this belief base it upon the undoubted strain which even the wealthiest nations are suffering. Certainly the increase of the various government debts has been staggering. . . .

We also have with us today a set of theorists who declare that America will soon become the financial center of the world. They may be correct, but the phenomena upon which they base their theory have been in existence almost too short a time to warrant permanent deductions. The theory is one highly flattering to ourselves, but it is not unlikely to prove another great illusion. To be sure, for the moment the world seems to be financially at America's feet. One evidence of this is the heavy discount at which the currency equivalents of the different belligerents have been selling in this market. Even the pound sterling last August fell to $4.50—which means that whereas, ordinarily, to buy £1000, one had to pay $4865, one could then buy the same amount of sterling with only $4500. And marks, francs, lire, kronen, and rubles have been at a far heavier discount.

Another evidence of financial ascendancy—and one more patent to the layman—lies in the considerable amount of foreign loans already taken by American investors. . . .

Of all these loans, the issue, jointly by Great Britain and France, of $500,000,000 bonds, has been far and away the most important single financial episode of the war, from America's point of view. Not only is it the largest sum ever raised in America at any one time, but it has carried in its train much controversy, many features touching upon the political as well as the commercial life of the nation. . . .

Moreover, before war had been many months under way it

had become apparent that for Americans, as individuals, to remain neutral in their thoughts and sympathies was beyond belief. Clear-thinking Americans were bound to become partisans for one side or for the other. . . . How could it have even been expected that an American business man, for instance, full of activity, ambitious for the upbuilding of his country's industry and commerce, could remain neutral? How could he ever forget that for a hundred and twenty-five years, up to the time of this war, France and England had given unlimited credit to commercial America, had lent us literally billions of dollars to help build our railways and factories, to aid in developing American industries? When the tables were turned and credit was sought from us, how could it be refused except on the theory that the American man of affairs is heartless as well as short-sighted? . . .

Finally, as to the future, though evidence is still wanting that the end of the war is in sight, we find ourselves already contemplating more new theories, possibly fresh illusions, as to the conditions that will obtain when the war is over. . . .

In thus picturing the industrial situation subsequent to the war, there are two general schools. One holds to the belief that business prostration in the now warring countries will be complete and prolonged; that, owing to the terrific destruction of wealth and capital, and to the continued necessities of the governments to meet the interest on their huge war loans, money will be in heavy demand and rates of interest high; that this demand will make itself felt all over the world, and will tend to curtail new enterprises everywhere; that here in the United States an early effect will be seen, and once more the pinch of poverty will be felt and depression in business be long continued. This school holds, furthermore, that the wastage of human life will have been so great that abroad there will be a dearth of labor, both skilled and unskilled; and that almost a generation, in point of time, will pass before this wastage of life will have been replaced and normal conditions of life and industry brought back. The cost of living, these theorists declare, will be maintained at a distressingly high figure, owing to the high cost of labor and to the continued heavy government taxes. The same school points out, too, that the belligerent nations will suffer greviously from the loss of a whole generation of educated and trained young men, who naturally would have been the leaders in science and industrial progress over the next two decades. The other school is much less pessimistic. It concedes a certain industrial languor and hesitation immediately following the war, but is confident that it will not be long continued. Its argument runs about as follows: The destruction of fixed capital (factories and equipment) will be found to have been greatly overestimated. To be sure, there has been destruction of villages by the wholesale, but, as compared with the total, the amount of fixed capital destroyed will be a small percentage. Of gold and securities there has been practically no loss. The process of industrial repair will begin at once, after the brief interval required for the returning soldier to beat his sword into a plowshare. Morever, there will be ample capital to serve, and at reasonable rates of interest. The reason therefor is twofold: first, because of the enormous savings resulting from the economies of the people at large; and, second, because of the vastly increased effectiveness in production of these people. It is pointed out that in all the warring nations habits of extraordinary thrift have been practised and are being permanently cultivated. And when populations aggregating two or three hundred million people are saving as never before, they build up capital almost as fast as even such a world war can waste it.

Furthermore, this school reiterates, the qualities of organization, of applied energy, and of determination, which the war is steadily cultivating, will render industry abroad a much more skilled tool than ever before. Then, indeed, will "scientific management" come to its real fruition. We may or may not see socialization of industry continued on an even greater scale than today in Germany and England. But in any event we shall see far better organization than ever before. And that means that American industry, labor, manufacture, will meet far more formidable competition than of old. Our markets will be flooded with products from an Old World made over, working at top speed, with an organization more aroused, skilled, and effective than ever before.

Who can say that either of these two schools of thought is

right or wrong? Time alone will reveal which, if either, of them has produced theories of value. If neither of them, then we shall again establish the precedent that only the unprecedented is to be expected. Whatever be the status after the war, it is plain that today, and for some years to come, there opens before the manufacturers and merchants of America unexampled opportunity for upbuilding. . . .

And with any such developments as I picture, with America lending her aid, in safe and orderly fashion, to rebuild the world, one must hope for a great increase in scientific attainment over here, for a great development of technical education, for a greater revival of the useful arts—a precursor, perhaps, of a great revival of learning and of the fine arts in America. It is being asserted of Americans today that, despite their donations to the suffering millions across the Atlantic, they are not thrilled with a deep and abiding sympathy for the spirit of self-sacrifice and heroism that is animating those struggling nations; that they are exulting too much in their own abundant, material prosperity. It seems a trite thing to say that all this wealth will be of no real use to the nation unless it aids in developing America's institutions, in educating and broadening her citizens; that all this material success will have gone for naught unless it adds to the nation's enlightenment and progress. Yet, without a revival of science and learning to illumine, to inspirit, and make them wise, business and finance can never fulfill their work of contributing substantially to the arts of peace and of civilization.

4   *The War-Boom Town in America*

*This brief account of the rapid transformation of Bridgeport, Con-
necticut, under the impact of war orders from Europe during the period
of neutrality provides a graphic illustration of the unexpected and far-
reaching consequences of the European war for industrial cities in the
United States well before the American intervention of 1917.*

Until last year Bridgeport was a comfortable manufacturing
town of about 115,000 people. It was a fair example of the
secondary commercial center in America, taking pride in its
solid prosperity, its moderate rate of advance, its leafy suburban
neighborhoods and family homes. Its peacetime industries were
various—among them bras and corsets and Singer sewing-
machines. The boom struck Bridgeport early in 1915. War orders
and a stream of European money flowed in. Existing factories
were rapidly adapted, and new ones were run up. One great
concern began to turn out heavy motor wagons; another was
making submarines. The population grew by some 50,000 in
less than twelve months. Men, especially young men, flocked
from all the places round into Bridgeport as a city of unlimited
opportunity. In the course of a few months a typical New
England town became one of the busiest hives of war industry
in America. The greatest single factor in this development has
been the Remington Arms Company, which during the summer
of last year laid the foundations of an immense factory on the
edge of the town. In October it has accommodation for 2,000
workpeople; by the beginning of this year about 15,000 were
employed in the range of a dozen or so huge uniform blocks.
About half the workers, maybe, are American born; the other
half come from the polyglot community of new Americans, fed,

SOURCE. "The War-Boom Town in America," *Living Age* (September 16,
1916), 290:751–753.

until the outbreak of war, by the unceasing immigrant stream.

The first assumption of the Remington Arms Company appears to have been that, since it was conferring upon Bridgeport the benefit of a fresh industry, bringing work and wealth to the town, the responsibility for housing and ordering the new population rested altogether with the city authorities. The consequences are not difficult to imagine. The problem of houseroom became unmanageable. Rents of houses and rooms leapt up. Land values were inflated. The owners and agents of real estate gathered a glorious harvest. It was estimated that at the end of 1914 the number of empty houses in Bridgeport and its suburbs was not far short of 2,000. A few months later there was not a house of any kind vacant nor a room to be obtained. Speculative builders, fearing a sudden ending to the prosperity, were reluctant to risk capital in housebuilding on a large scale, and accordingly the Remington Company was forced into action. In addition to other housing schemes, it set about building dormitories for about 4,000 women workers. It has not yet, however, addressed itself to the provision of schools and recreative centers. These latter, especially, are a very urgent necessity for a community of young men and women, removed from their normal surroundings and with plenty of money to spend, so that they overflow all the existing places of entertainment. The economic conditions, especially the sharp competition for workmen between the firms and the abundance of money, made a soil favorable to labor disputes. The record of Bridgeport in this regard is quite extraordinary. During a period of two and a half months last summer fifty-five strikes occurred. They resulted in notable gains to the workers, who were able to secure improved rates of wages and a standard working day. Bridgeport is now an eight-hour town.

PACIFISM AND PREPAREDNESS

5   *Jane Addams*
What War Is Destroying

*Women reacted quickly against the prospect of American intervention
in the war. In a speech before a conference called to organize the
Women's Peace Party, a famous social worker discusses the presumed
sensibility of women to the "treasuring of life," stronger among females
than men. She calls for a feminine revolt against the war, linking up the
crusade for women's rights with pacifism.*

Thousands of people in this United States and Europe had
become so convinced that the sanctity of life was an accepted
tenet of civilization that they deemed war had become forever
impossible. This belief has been rudely overturned, and we
are now at the foot of the ladder, beginning again to establish
the belief that human life is sacred above all else that the planet
contains.

I do not assert that women are better than men—even in the
heat of suffrage debates I have never maintained that—but we
would all admit that there are things concerning which women
are more sensitive than men, and that one of these is the treasuring of life. I would ask you to consider with me five aspects
concerning this sensitiveness which war is rapidly destroying:

SOURCE. Jane Addams, "What War Is Destroying," *Advocate of Peace* (1915),
77:64-65.

The first is the *protection* of human life. The advanced nations know very accurately, and we have begun to know in America, how many children are needlessly lost in the first years of infancy. Measures inaugurated for the prevention of infant mortality were slowly spreading from one country to another. All that effort has been scattered to the winds by the war. No one is now pretending to count the babies who are dying throughout the villages and country-sides of the warring nations. We know only that a sudden rise in the infant death rate was the first casualty of the war to be reported, beginning when the troops were mobilizing.

The second aspect is the *nurture* of human life. From the time a soldier is born to the moment he marches in his uniform to be wantonly destroyed, it is largely the women of his household who have cared for him. War overthrows not only the work of the mother, the nurse, and the teacher, but at the same time ruthlessly destroys the very conception of the careful nurture of life.

The third aspect is the *fulfillment* of human life. Every woman who cares for a little child fondly throws her imagination forward to the time when he shall have become a great and heroic man. Every baby is thus made human, and is developed by the hope and expectation which surrounds him. But no one in Europe, in the face of war's destruction, can consider the fulfillment of life, and we are feeling the reaction of war's ideals in America every day.

The fourth aspect is the *conservation* of human life; that which expresses itself in the state care of dependent children, in old-age pensions; the sentiment which holds that every scrap of human life is so valuable that the human family cannot neglect a feeble child without risking its own destruction. At this moment none of the warring countries of Europe can cherish the aged and infirm. The state cannot give care to its dependents when thousands of splendid men are dying each day. Little children and aged people are dying, too, in some countries in the proportion of five to one soldier killed on the field, but the nation must remain indifferent to their suffering.

And last of all is that which we call the *ascent* of human life;

that which leads a man to cherish the hope that the next generation shall advance beyond the generation in which he lives; that generous glow we all experience when we see that those coming after us are equipped better than we have been. The hope for the ascent of life is at the basis of social progress. We know that Europe at the end of this war will not begin to build where it left off; we know that it will begin generations behind the point it had reached when the war began.

If we admit that this sensitiveness for human life is stronger in women than in men because women have been responsible for the care of the young and the aged and those who need special nurture, it is certainly true that this sensitiveness developed in women carries with it an obligation.

Once before in the history of the world, in response to this sensitiveness, women called a halt to the sacrifice of human life, although it then implied the abolition of a religious observance long believed to be right and necessary. In the history of one nation after another it was the mothers who first protested that their children should no longer be slain as living sacrifices upon the altars of the tribal gods, although the national leaders contended that human sacrifice, bound up with all the traditions of religion and patriotism, could not be abolished. . . .

Many of us believe that throughout this round world of ours there are thousands of men and women who have become convinced that the sacrifice of life in warfare is unnecessary and wasteful. It is possible that if women in Europe—in the very countries which are now at war—receive a message from the women of America solemnly protesting against this sacrifice, they may take courage to formulate their own. At any rate, those of us assembled here will state as intelligently as we can this international revolt among thinking men and women.

6   *Was Jesus Christ a Pacifist?*

*As soon as the war began, religious proponents of pacifism marshalled
arguments against those co-religionists who advanced justification for
violence. A favorite approach was to discuss the scriptural basis for the
image of Christ as the Prince of Peace.*

It is charged against the Christian Church that it condoned
the ideals and policies which ended in this war. There is evidence that this same Christian Church is now "blessing" the
war which it did nothing to prevent. There are other evidences
that it is now planning to exploit the tragedy of it to its own
interest. There is no systematic, general, or even sporadic attempt on the part of the Christian Church anywhere to pro-   ·
mote the ideals and policies of an international organization.
There is little evidence that the Christian Church has, during
the last generation, done any concrete thing to prevent the present war. Priests in all lands, belligerent and neutral, pray to
the same Christ to "bless" their troops, their rulers, and the
whole infernal paraphernalia that brought on the present
situation. Cardinal Mercier, of Belgium, for example, delivered
a most eloquent address in Brussels on the 21st of last July, on
the occasion of the Belgian National Holiday. One pathetic
thing about this very great address was the way in which the
eminent Cardinal faced both ways upon the question of retali-
ation. He said first, with great tenderness: "Our lips, purified
by the fire of Christian charity, do not utter any hate. To hate
is to take the misfortune of others for our goal and to delight
in it. However great our griefs may be, we do not wish any evil
to those who inflict them upon us. National concord with us is
allied to universal fraternity." But His Eminence then turned to
the ancient authority of St. Thomas of Aquino, and pointed out

SOURCE. "Was Jesus Christ a Pacifist?" *Advocate of Peace* (1916), **78**:287–288.

the necessity for "public prosecution," calling for a kind of "public vengeance," even though it "may irritate the sentimentality of a weak soul," and spoke approvingly of "an avenging weapon of slighted right."

And so again we are confronted with the old question of the attitude of Jesus Christ toward war. Did he or did he not teach the legitimacy of military force as a means of settling disputes? Was Jesus Christ a pacifist?

Now we have no disposition to quibble about this question. Whether God and Christ are or are not what we make them is irrelevant. It may be true that if one's nature demands a belief in a war-Christ, one will find such a Christ in spite of reason, exegesis, or fact. But how was it with the Christ of the New Testament?

It is disquieting that he left us no direct word upon such an important matter as "preparedness." There must have been Plattsburgs in those days, but Jesus does not refer to them. The Roman "National Guard" drew no comment from him. We of today are considerably stirred up about education, art, science, business, politics, nationalism. Jesus had nothing to say about any of these great problems.

Stranger still, he proceeded to give voice to certain utterances which seem to have a militaristic ring. In the 24th chapter of Matthew, for instance, we are told that "Ye shall hear of wars and rumors of wars: see that ye be not troubled: for these things must come to pass, but the end is not yet. For nation shall rise against nation, and kingdom against kingdom." Thus we are told that Jesus taught the inevitableness of war. And this in spite of what he goes on to add: "All these things are the beginning of trouble. . . . And many false prophets shall rise, and shall lead many astray. . . . But he that endureth to the end, the same shall be saved."

Again, in Matthew 10:34, we have the familiar words: "Think not that I came to send peace on the earth: I came not to send peace, but a sword." This is quoted by the militarist as final and conclusive. But in this case the infinitive *to send* is, as has often been pointed out, an infinitive not of purpose, but of result—a forecast of what was to happen to the disciples, not of what the disciples were to do unto others. The conception is figurative throughout, and has no relation whatsoever to international war.

And then in the 11th chapter of Mark appears the account of the temple episode. Nowhere, however, in this, the most authentic account of the four, do we find that Jesus had any kind of an instrument in his hand. His aim was simply to oust the desecrating men and animals from the Holy Temple. The demonstration was a demonstration not of physical but of moral force. It is interesting to note that Matthew and Luke, both of whom tell this same story, agree substantially with Mark. It is only in John, "the interpreter," the least historical of the four, that we read of a "scourge of cords." But even here there is no evidence that Jesus struck a man. Anyhow, no mere whip in the hands of a lone and weary man would have driven an unwilling crowd before. it.

The arguments for war based upon the teachings of Jesus are best described by one Shakespeare:

> *"What damned error but some sober brow to bless it,*
> *And approve it with a Text."*

Jesus everywhere was opposed to physical force. He had nothing but rebuke for the one who smote the servant of the high priest. His behavior under temptation in the Wilderness, his own analysis of himself on the way to Caesarea-Philippi, his supreme self-mastery in the Garden of Gethsemane, at Golgotha, showed him superior to physical force, showed him, indeed, surcharged with a super-force, the force of love, of service, of sacrifice, of gentleness, of persuasion and consolation, the very force that won eight million followers within two centuries and overcame the Roman world. There was nothing in him of the camp or of the modern emphasis that States rest only on guns and battleships. The heart and faith and message of this man was of peace. The heart and faith and message of the Christian Church for its first two hundred years, said by some to be the only Christian Church which we have ever had, was the heart and faith and message of peace. The supreme fact of the Christian ethic was then, and ought to be now, that Jesus Christ was a pacifist.

7   Paul U. Kellogg
A Bill of Particulars: Items in an
International Policy for America

A leading advocate of the "social justice" Progressives speaks out in behalf of neutrality and internationalism, the two-sided Wilsonian formula prior to 1917, presenting the arguments used by anti-preparedness groups to counteract the views of those who urged increases in the armed forces.

My belief is that what great numbers of Americans want to know is not merely the size of the war establishment we are asked to commit ourselves to—but its course—what policies go with it? What relation has it not merely to efficiency and to the larger programme of social preparedness, but to parallel policies such as will stave off the curse of militarism, such as will prevent war; and even more to those principles America is to stand for, both in its own might and in laying the framework for a new understanding among nations?

Mr. Hughes laid his finger on the first of these in his telegram of acceptance—efficiency. We should like to see him press it further. We want to know not merely the size of our proposed military establishment, but whether it is to be superimposed on the present unsound and wasteful system. We want to know whether it is to be accompanied by a programme of social and industrial upbuilding, with which, as the events in Europe have shown, military preparedness is a thatch of straw. None of the leading platforms carries conviction that its farmers grasped the revolutionary but specific policies which the British under Lloyd George have found it necessary to resort to in mobilizing in-

SOURCE: Paul U. Kellogg, "A Bill of Particulars: Items in an International Policy for America," *Nation* (August 3, 1916), **103**:1, Section 2.

dustrial resources, in controlling transportation and raw materials, and in grappling with the parasitic profit interests in
war—still less those deep-reaching policies for developing economic and human strength which, since the Franco-Prussian
War, have fitted the Teutonic peoples to withstand all Europe
in arms against them.

We want to know what counterbalancing forces we may count
on to hamstring the forces of militarism which, unchecked, have
engulfed the most liberal governments of Europe. In spite of
warnings spoken by a foremost statesman of England against
plunging into extraordinary military expenditures (at a time
when the clearest thinkers of all nations are hoping that the
end of the war would see the beginning of a process of disarmament), there is no slightest word in any platform that would
commit us to taking the initiative or even to cooperating in
such a process. In spite of Mr. Borah's scathing denunciation
in the Senate of the grants to the National Guard as a scheme
bound to build up a political-military machine more insidious
than the greatest of standing armies, there is no criticism of that
plan in the Republican platform. In spite of the known agency
of great profit-taking initiatives as provocatives of war, no platform challenges them in the spirit with which progressive leaders
of all parties have assailed other strongholds of privilege. In
spite of the fact that our recent military and naval appropriations bills transcend all appropriations in the past to education,
public health, agricultural demonstration, the Bureau of Mines
and the like, I find no clear-cut insistence in any platform that
such constructive governmental activities shall not be starved
out by the drains for army and navy.

We want to know how much energy Mr. Hughes proposes
to invest not only in preparation for war but in preventing war.
We have in mind entirely specific and practical measures to this
end. We have in mind the proposals, dormant since the Taft
Administration, which would give Federal courts jurisdiction
in all cases involving treaty rights of aliens resident in the
United States and which would prevent any single State from
involving the whole country in needless war. We have in mind
various practical suggestions, such as a ratio basis for regulating

immigration, such as would clear away the dormant friction with Japan. We have in mind the systematical pushing of our protests against British interference with trade and mails—with anything like the vigor with which we maintained the rights of life at sea against the Germans—so as to remove the impending mistrust in our good faith and neutrality by the German people. We have in mind the belated undertaking of a joint commission to work out an adequate policing of the Mexican border.

The Republican plank calling for a "world court," brief and unsatisfactory though it was, is the sole reference in the three platforms to the machinery of law by which a great alternative to war might be devised. Mr. Roosevelt and Mr. Straus have played notable parts in the Hague conferences. Mr. Root and Mr. Choate were our two most distinguished figures there. Mr. Taft is president of the League to Enforce Peace. It would seem that with these outstanding precedents to draw on, the Republican party might feel sure-footed in affording us constructive leadership in line with proposals which for months past have been put out by responsible groups in both neutral and belligerent countries, urging the further development of international courts to settle judiciable disputes; urging conferences of conciliation to adjust international bargains; urging international agreements to bring all such cases before court or conference; urging united action against the nation which refuses so to do; urging international councils to build up our body of international law.

Yet there is no hint in any platform of instituting an international naval force as a step toward these ends or as an alternative to competitive naval armaments; much less is there hint of employing economic compulsion as a modern substitute, or even of pledging our friendly interest to the nation which in any dispute declares for negotiation rather than war as the means for settlement. The way is clear for new leadership in this well-explored field.

The Democrats have denounced making material interests an excuse for asserting superior power against the fundamental rights of smaller states in managing their own internal affairs.

They have set up the lives of citizens and the claims of humanity as of greater moment than commercial claims with respect to our rights on the high seas. They have come out of a complete security of peaceful navigation and for the common and unhindered use of the high seas by the merchant craft of all nations.

This is only a beginning and, of course, largely negative. No amount of international governmental machinery may be presupposed to keep the world at peace or to make that peace tolerable, unless it be shot through with such principles of democracy as will call for the protection of the weaker peoples, no less than of the weaker nations, in their culture, language, religion, and the like; shot through with such principles of conservation as will make colonialism no longer a scourge to backward races and a spur toward war among their exploiters.

The formulation of an American public policy along such constructive lines would make itself felt among the peoples at war as something to tie to in the midst of their travail; something that offered strength and reserves of faith in the new world that could be counted upon for democracy, for justice, for liberty, come what may; something to bolster the courage that will be needed to build a new order out of the wreck of war.

Nearer at home and nearer in point of time, such a leadership would gather to itself the forces which, at the end of two full years of war, are groping toward action as against inaction, toward an American policy which, unlike either a do-nothing neutrality or a blind national defense, would be affirmative and fired with a vision for mankind.

8 *John Hays Hammond*
The Issues of 1916

The author, a well-known businessman, presents a comprehensive argument for "preparedness" in response to the European crisis, arguing not only for an augmented national defense but also for unprecedented national discipline to cope with novel changes wrought by the war. The article served as a campaign document for Charles Evans Hughes, the Republican candidate for President in 1916.

The coming twelve months hold the United States in the balance. The thought of the world as well as the governments of the world are in process of change. Europe is in the labor of a new birth. We do not know where the new thought will lead and we do not know what the new Europe will be like. But we do know that at the close of this Titanic struggle Europe will be confronted with dire poverty, and in these desperate straits she will become more formidable than ever in industrial competition with the rest of the world.

While Europe is thus changing, we in the United States are going more or less blissfully forward to the accumulation of vast wealth—obtained not by our striking efficiency but because a large portion of the world has been taken from the mill and put in the trenches. Our present prosperity has come upon us as suddenly as summer rain and we have had as much to do with its coming as we have to do with the coming of the rain.

The war over, we must meet Europe in the battle for supremacy. We cannot decline the ordeal unless we are willing to abdicate our present high position among the nations of the world. We cannot stand still. We must progress or retrogress. We have changed from an agricultural to a manufacturing

SOURCE. John Hays Hammond, "The Issues of 1916," *Forum* (1916), **56**: 22–32.

people and our products are greater than the home consumption; we must have a foreign outlet. We cannot alter our economic development and therefore we should be prepared to meet all comers in all fields. We are not now thus prepared and, unless we clearly see what is before us and adjust ourselves to meet new conditions, our prosperity will vanish as quickly as it came.

The vital American undertaking is this: To make a nation, united and purposeful, with a coordination of all forces to realize the best that is in us.

The grave, fundamental problems that are before us, as a nation, to solve group themselves under these broad heads:

1. The obtaining and sustaining of an adequate military and naval defence in harmony with our institutions.

2. The safeguarding of our home markets and the extension of our trade into foreign markets.

3. The coordination of our government and our industry upon a basis that will eliminate waste and gain the highest efficiency in each.

4. The safeguarding of our nation against war by strong international relations and a firm, well-considered foreign policy.

It is unfortunate that the solution of these great economic problems is not entirely dissociated from party politics. Problems essentially economic in import and vital to the welfare of the entire nation are too often determined on strictly political lines. These questions are, in a large measure, settled by politicians upon the stump, not by business men in boards of trade.

NATIONAL DEFENCE

Preparedness—preparedness against war is one of the great, if not indeed the most important of problems today, demanding the immediate attention of our National Congress.

The present unspeakable conflict in Europe has brought with it a vivid realization of how unintelligent our present methods are, how pitifully we lack in the field of international relations the most elementary machinery for the redress of grievances and for the avoidance of conflict such as is provided in the internal organization of the State. No individual is safeguarded; and the Nation is defenceless when "might becomes right."

That we have not the power to defend ourselves is now universally admitted—reluctantly admitted, it is true—by some whose duty it was to apprise the Nation early of the fact so it should no longer be lulled into a feeling of security based upon misrepresentations which unwisely considered political expediency rather than the welfare of the Nation.

Only two objections can be urged against military preparedness. The ultra-pacifist, peace-at-any-price class oppose it because they fear that our Nation might develop a spirit of imperialism, jingoism, or a militaristic mania which would tend to provoke rather than to prevent war.

Against this contention is the irrefutable argument of the cosmopolitan character of our population which tends to conservatism in international relations, the unimpeachable tradition of the pacific policy of our Nation, and the fact that we have no occasion and no ambition for territorial expansion.

If we Americans cannot depend upon our own self-restraint, if we cannot entrust to our own people the exercise of might for the reasons advanced against preparedness, what convincing argument can there be that governments of other nations, possessing superior power, might not abuse that power when international controversies arise?

I believe that *the mania for peace at any price* and unpreparedness *is a far greater peril to the Nation than the mania for militarism.*

There is a second objection: the cost of national defence. The estimated wealth of our Nation is upwards of one hundred and eighty-five billion dollars. It is the opinion of recognized authorities that the expenditure of less than one billion dollars, in addition to our present naval and military budget, would provide a navy and an army that would afford the Nation adequate protection against any probable contingency—that is, an expenditure not exceeding the cost of a few weeks' war on the part of any of the present belligerents, an expenditure far less than would be inflicted on our country by a first-class Power within a few weeks of the outbreak of war. And therefore, while all thoughtful men admit that the maintenance of great armies and navies is a futile expenditure in that it serves no useful purpose, that it is a prodigal expenditure in that it diverts enormous sums of money from the alleviation of human suffering to which it could otherwise be applied, nevertheless, *I believe* that under existing conditions it would be indefensible, indeed execrable parsimony to oppose national defence solely because of the expense involved.

I believe that time, in carrying out our programme of national defence, is of supreme importance not only to safeguard against menace but to enable our Nation to exercise an influence in the Council of Nations commensurate with our position among the nations of the world.

THE SAFEGUARDING OF OUR TRADE

With a rapidly increasing population and especially a rapidly increasing number of wage earners, we must extend our industrial activities, but we must not lose sight of the fact that over-extension in industry inevitably causes depression in times of business recession. Authorities agree that we are now rapidly approaching the limit—the point of saturation, in our domestic markets, insofar as demands under normal conditions are concerned.

It is obvious, therefore, that we must either curtail the capacity of our factories (which would result in throwing out of employment millions of wage earners and the disorganization of complementary industries) or we must depend upon the exploitation of foreign countries for the relief of our congested home markets.

In foreign markets we meet our great trade rivals who, by years of experience and by the expenditure of colossal sums of money, have obtained a firm foothold in the markets we seek. Therefore to compete successfully with these nations we must secure for ourselves every advantage we can derive from the most efficient exploitation of our national industries, fostered by constructive legislation at home and promoted by able commercial diplomacy abroad. This has been notably the policy of

Germany and its success is evidenced by the unparalleled strides she has made in the development of her great foreign commerce. There should be, in my opinion, a readjustment of our commercial treaties as soon after the war as possible to enable our Government to make separate treaties with the different nations to our mutual advantage, giving us an adequate return for any concessions we may make as to the admission of their exports. This is, admittedly, dollar diplomacy—but good, honorable, legitimate business; the Pecksniffian pinheads to the contrary notwithstanding. . . .

COORDINATION OF GOVERNMENT AND INDUSTRY

One of the great problems before the American people is how to increase efficiency—coordinated efficiency—in industry, in the political administration of City, State and Nation, and in our domestic affairs. As a nation we are characterized by prodigality and have, as yet, devoted little scientific endeavor to the curtailment of waste—waste in the consumption of millions of dollars yearly by preventable fires, waste in the development of our great timber tracts, our mines, our farms, economic waste from excessive industrial accidents, waste in our domestic affairs— waste in every phase of our national life.

The fundamental requisite for successful competition for the world's markets is efficiency, which means low cost production. It is well to disabuse our minds of the cherished delusion of the tremendous "superiority of the American laborer" "Yankee ingenuity," and "American machinery" over that of all foreign countries. This superiority in productive efficiency no longer obtains in the same degree as formerly for the reason that technical training abroad, coupled with the introduction of American machinery, has already minimized the advantage that America formerly had. For their self-protection American wage earners will be compelled to increase their efficiency to render possible the maintenance of the American standard of living while lowering the cost of production to enable our country to compete successfully in foreign commerce. . . .

There has been much unintelligent prejudice, partly inspired for political purposes, against what we call "Big Business," but the people of the country ought by this time to be convinced that unless our industries can be developed on large-scale production, as is the practice of our great European trade rivals, we shall be seriously handicapped in our quest for foreign markets. England permits, France encourages, and Germany sometimes even compels combinations in the interest of the industry involved and of the general public. The policy of Germany has been to promote the prosperity of its industries, not to invoke the technicalities of laws formulated by unpractical theorists in political economy, as in America.

In this country competition is regarded by many of our political leaders as the "life of trade." As a matter of fact, competition, when unduly stimulated, often works irreparable injury to industrial communities by the resulting lower wages, by fluctuations in prices which depress business, and by the loss of investments. "Reasonable stability in prices is the basis of prosperous trade". . . .

It is by stimulated misunderstanding that the latent savagery, common to all men, is aroused and the passions so engendered, when unrestrained, lead to war; and the vaulting ambitions of selfish and incompetent statesmanship of those shaping the destinies of nations are at fault, rather than the peoples of the nations themselves. It seems unbelievable that the cooperation of the great intellects of the world, exercising but a modicum of that ingenuity expended in the invention of terrible engines of destruction, should not be able to devise a plan by which the nations of the world would submit their controversies to a Supreme Court of Nations and thus relegate to the scrap-heap of progressive civilization the settlement of disputes by the arbitrament of arms.

9   *John Grier Hibben*
The Colleges and National Defense

The President of Princeton University presents the case for military
training in the colleges and universities, indicating the positive virtues of
such training as well as refuting the arguments raised against the idea.

The problem of military preparedness is of particular interest
in its bearings upon the young men of the higher schools and
colleges of our country. I do not believe in the idea that we
should endeavor to make our students soldiers, or to prepare
them for a soldier's career, but it seems to me a matter of very
serious consideration whether it is not wise to provide for them
some opportunity to secure a minimum amount of knowledge
which will make their services immediately valuable in the time
of a great national emergency. In our colleges generally the
undergraduates are taught to regard the privileges of an education as creating certain extraordinary responsibilities on their
part to make their lives serviceable directly or indirectly to the
nation. With this spirit largely prevailing throughout our country it is natural that our young men should consider among
their other responsibilities that of preparing themselves in some
slight measure at least to defend their land in the possible
event of war.

It is certain that our college graduates and undergraduates as
well would naturally be expected to enlist in their country's
service if there should arise any necessity of a call for volunteers.
If war should actually occur, forced upon us against our will and
desire, it would not be difficult of course to secure volunteers,
and although many thousands would rally to the colors with

SOURCE. John G. Hibben, "The Colleges and National Defense," *Independent*
(1915), **82**:532–533.

admirable spirit and enthusiasm, nevertheless they would be untrained, undisciplined and withal densely ignorant of military
theory and practise. It is on this account that the college man
should have some little knowledge of military procedure so that
he may be of assistance, at the first outbreak of hostilities, to the
recruiting and training officers. He could help at a time when
help would be most needed. The educated man at such a crisis
should be able to offer something more than a willing spirit. He
should have the knowledge as well as the disposition to serve his
country's need. Courage will not compensate for ignorance.

The great argument for unpreparedness is that after war is
declared the volunteer army can be trained for the needed defense of the country, but this policy in our past history has
always increased the initial horrors of war and has caused a
wholly unnecessary prolongation of the period of war and an
indefinite postponement of the return of peace. To send our
untrained youth into battle against a highly trained and efficient
military machine is not war; it is slaughter, most cruel and in-
excusable, and he who assumes the responsibility of such a procedure is nothing less than a murderer. It is in order to save
ourselves from such a bitter and humiliating experience that I
feel it is incumbent upon our young men to prepare themselves
for their part in the common obligation of averting a national
catastrophe. There is a difference which must be kept in mind
between a possibility which is one of fancy and purely academic
and a possibility which has a reasonable chance of being realized.
The possibility of war is of the latter type and therefore must
be reckoned with in all plans for the futures.

There are two ways in which so great a people as ourselves
may prepare for the defense of our country. One is the concentration of military knowledge and experience in a large
standing army, and the other is the diffusion of military knowledge and experience widely throughout the entire nation. What
I would emphasize is the need of military strength without
military display, a reserve power without the diminution of
economic efficiency and the serious drain upon our resources
which a large standing army necessitates. If we can secure military knowledge and skill in a potential rather than actual form,

we will avoid all the dangers of a self-sufficient and arrogant militarism. That which creates an aggressive war spirit is the elaboration of the war machine and the subordination of all other interests in a nation to it. Military strength, however, which is available but not visible, and therefore incapable of ostentatious display, will enable us to meet any critical emergency which may arise and at the same time will leave us free from the domination of a militaristic caste and militaristic policy.

In the line of this idea I urge that kind of instruction in our colleges which can be carried on without any armory, or arms, or uniform, and where there will be no display whatsoever of the external symbols of war, but where instruction may be carried on through lectures and the study of the problems of tactics in the field. We have planned to do this at Princeton and to have the course an optional one. It is to be an extracurriculum activity and is to be under the control of the undergraduates themselves. General Leonard Wood has promised to cooperate in furnishing officers from time to time to give lectures and tactical excursions through the surrounding country. To supplement instruction of this kind an opportunity is given to all of the students of the higher schools and colleges of our country to attend the summer camps which have been planned by our Government....

Several objections may be urged to the ideas which I have presented. One is that instruction in military procedures creates a taste for war. This in my opinion represents a very superficial view of the matter. The causes which produce a desire for war on the part of the people lie much deeper; they spring from those darker sources of national greed, the love of conquest, and the disregard of treaty obligations and the rights of a weaker nation. The desire to prepare oneself intelligently to serve his country's need at a time of possible peril does not in itself create the aggressive spirit of war. It serves rather to emphasize the idea of the seriousness of war and the serious responsibility which any nation assumes which chooses to act as aggressor in so desperate an enterprise.

Another objection is that the exhibition of interest in military affairs by our colleges at this particular time will be surely mis-

interpreted; it will give the impression at least that war is one
of the necessities of national experience. And it is still further
urged that the total indifference concerning everything that per-
tains to war on the part of great intellectual centers is in itself
a protest against warfare of any kind whatsoever. The only
justification of such a point of view is the theory that war can
never be justifiable and that there can be no emergency which
would compel our country to take arms against a foreign foe,
even though our land might be invaded.

It is said, also, that if we busy ourselves with military instruction it will prevent our colleges and those of us who represent them from identifying ourselves with the peace movement of the day. I do not believe this. I feel that if our young
men wisely inform themselves concerning the possible military
duties which they may be called upon to perform it will in no
wise work against the desire to maintain peace in our land and
to bring about the day of universal peace for all the earth. Preparedness and a desire for peace are not mutually exclusive
ideas. It is not only illogical but morally wrong to assume that
all who believe in a wise preparedness are therefore naturally to
be regarded as so much inflammable material at the mere suggestion of war.

A fourth objection is that it will be time for us to prepare
for an emergency when it comes; that the nation will prove its
spirit and power in the time of its danger. This idea is folly.
All the experiences of the past in our country and in foreign
lands prove that such a fallacy must be paid for dearly in the
needless and wanton sacrifice of the best blood of the youth of
our nation, to say nothing of the possible horrors which may
come to our defenseless women and children.

Finally it has been urged that any effort at this time to prepare ourselves for any future emergency will be a manifest dis-
advantage to our nation when the day of peace comes to Europe.
I do not believe this. As we have no desire to increase our army
to any conspicuous degree whatsoever, this objection seems to
me to have little force. Our army could be doubled and quad-
rupled and still its members be such that if all the standing
armies of Europe were reduced to a like basis it would result

substantially in a general European disarmament. Our influence can be exercized only in one way, by our stout and determined insistence upon the respect of treaty obligations, upon the rights of weaker nations, and upon a central world power which will enforce the decrees of a supreme court of international arbitration. This is the field of our influence. The fact that we may endeavor to make proper preparation to defend our rights and liberties as a nation will in no sense prevent us from showing to the world a right disposition to serve the nations of the earth in the cause of our common humanity. The only thing that Europe will resent and will be justified in resenting on our part is a smug complacency or the evidence of any desire to profit as a nation through the distress and disaster which must inevitably befall these warring peoples in the wake of this, the greatest of all world calamities.

10   Robert Cromwell Root
Military Training in Schools

The author vigorously enumerates the arguments offered against military education in the schools.

1.   The school courses are already too full; therefore no other course should be added. . . .
2.   Military training has not enough educational value to replace any subject that rightfully belongs in the school courses of study. . . .
3.   The supposed benefits of military training can be secured more effectively by other means: the gymnasium and outdoor games and athletics. . . .

SOURCE. Robert Cromwell Root, "Military Training in Schools: Twelve Objections," *Advocate of Peace* (1916), **78**:109–110.

4. The regulations generally, if not invariably, used in military drill were prepared for adults and not for boys. The California law of 1915 states that U. S. Army regulations are to be used in drilling high-school cadets. This is manifestly an absurd requirement. . . .

5. The girls, even more than the boys, need the physical development supposed to be derived from military training; but the system thus far in use wholly ignores this greater need of the girls. . . .

6. For all except a few officers in command, military training develops a blind, unthinking obedience. "Their's not to reason why, Their's but to do and die"—pitiable "Six Hundred"! For the rank and file, military training represses individuality . . . in the boys at the very time these qualities should be developed. Hence, for the rank and file, military drill prepares the boys to be mere imitators and automatons instead of self-reliant leaders of their fellow-men. Since military training . . . has not enough educational value to replace any other subject, and since the supposed benefits may be more effectively secured by other accessible, practical means, and since one-half of the school population is wholly ignored by this system, it therefore seems to be perfectly clear that the actual value of military training is practically nil and should have no place in our school courses. . . .

8. To establish military drill in our schools would, in the boys' minds, place the emphasis on might and not on right. It would very strongly imply that might should be the first instead of the last line of defense. . . .

9. Military training in the public schools fosters a suspicion and distrust of other nations. Acting on the fictitious plea of "national necessity," a "national enemy" must be found. This engenders international hatred—a long step toward war. . . .

10. Military training in the public schools is not necessary in order to teach patriotism or to provide for national defense. Military drill may lead to efficiency on the parade ground or to skill at target practice, but it does not necessarily develop the spirit of patriotism. Real patriotism is of the spirit—of qualities of mind and heart; hence it is not acquired by evolutions on the

drill ground or by shooting at a target. True patriotism grows out of character. It requires a patriot to live a clean, strong life for his country quite as much as it requires one to be ready to die in defense of his country....

11. The moral danger. The laws of the community and of the State forbid the boy to carry arms. He knows that the man who assaults his fellow-man with a deadly weapon is tried in court for his liberty or his life. He goes to Sunday school and learns the command: "Thou shalt not kill." He attends church and hears that he must "do unto others as he would have others do unto him," and then he joins the cadet corps and is trained with gun and sword in the art of killing his fellow-men! Then we wonder why our boys have such hazy ideas on moral questions! We wonder why our boys are so often lacking in clear vision, clear reasoning, and right action....

12. The school system and the war system have nothing in common. We should be unalterably opposed to military drill in our public schools because it would join in close partnership the finest thing that American civilization has given to humanity —our free public schools, the hope of democracy—with war, the most barbaric, inhuman, and un-Christian system ever inflicted upon a struggling world.

Let us teach our boys that law and order must replace war and the "Golden Rule" replace the law of hate and martial conflict.

ONSET OF BELLIGERENCY

11   *Sydney Brooks*
Impressions of America at War

*An English journalist records his impressions of the United States as
its people moved from peace to war early in 1917, particularly the reaction of the Middle West. Brooks presents a shrewd analysis of President Wilson's political method, which included a vital identification of
the Allied cause with the principles of democracy.*

What I think has most struck me has geen the gradual awakening of the "plain people" to the realities of the German political
character. I was a good deal in Ohio and Michigan after Count
Bernstorff's dismissal, after the publication of the Zimmermann
note, but before the declaration of war. Are Ohio and Michigan
to be reckoned as forming part of the Middle West? I do not
know. But if they are, then the Middle West as a separate and
distinctive section of the Union, with a point of view all its
own, indifferent to the war, indifferent to preparedness, indifferent to what a New York paper called "the abstraction
known as national honor," is and always has been simply a fig-
ment of the Eastern imagination. I had often doubted whether
it really existed. I could never quite persuade myself that so
robust and virile a portion of the United States, one that had

SOURCE. Sydney Brooks, "Impressions of America at War," *North American
Review* (1917), **205**:673–682.

responded with such emphatic resolution only a few years before to Mr. Roosevelt's leadership, was really as dead and as
plethoric as my New York friends made out. That it was remote
from the war and perhaps a shade overengrossed in its own
affairs and rather too much preoccupied with the little State
point of view, was true enough. But there are many other parts
of the United States, and I dare say of all countries not actually
in the war or on the very fringe of it, of which as much could
truthfully be said. The tug of intimate, personal things is
something that only a counterstrain of abnormal potency can
resist.

But the good people of Ohio and Michigan, as I went among
them in February and March, seemed to me to have far more
interest in the European struggle than the average Englishman
or Frenchman would have in, let us say, a civil war in China.
The men and women who one would expect to be pro-Ally in
New York or Philadelphia or Providence were not less so in
Toledo and Dayton and Saginaw; and, if there was less general
discussion of the war in the press, on the streets, at the dinner
table, and in the railway cars, I found none of that pervasive
apathy I had been led to expect. It was my own fault entirely
that I should have been surprised. I ought to have known that
New York is the worst of all possible watch-towers from which
to spy out the currents of American emotion. I should have
remembered that it knows about as much of its own hinterland
as a Londoner of what is going on and being felt and thought
in Manitoba. So far as I could judge all that Ohio and Michigan
needed—all, indeed, that the whole of the United States needed
—was a lead. The ordinary citizen one encountered had, I
found, been somewhat nettled by the assumption that he cared
little for his country's security or good name; and to repeat in
his presence that famous phrase about being too proud to fight
was to evoke on the spot an outburst of most satisfying Americanism. Here and there one came across the trail of the professorial type of pacifist. One soon found that he could safely
be left for local opinion to deal with. After the Zimmermann
revelations, which unquestionably unsealed many eyes, there
was no room for any sort of doubt as to where the Middle West
stood. People saw and said that Germany had become a world-

nuisance which America would have to play her part in abating. But there was no war-fever. Indeed the student of national temper and psychology could hardly wish for a more striking contrast than that between the America of 1917 and the America of 1898. . . . America has lived much in the last twenty years; and the poise and dignity of the national bearing during the past two trying months have been one of the most impressive features of the whole crisis. . . .

Certainly I got the impression that if in February and March the Middle West had been asked to give the President a lead, it neither would nor could have responded to the request. The situation was beyond it. It had not the material for forming a judgment. Its inclination was all on the side not of giving a lead but of getting one. Clay in the potter's hand, it had no thought of being anything else. The President could have moulded it whichever way he pleased. Had he thrown a veil of resounding generalities over a policy of uncompromising pacifism and announced flatly that, though he had broken off diplomatic relations, under no circumstances would he go to war, a great body of Middle Western opinion would have rallied at once to his support. Had he set to work to rouse public opinion and give it a belligerent twist, a still larger body of opinion, in my judgment, would instantly have gathered round him. But as he chose to do neither, the news and sentiments of an uninstructed and leaderless populace were split into a hundred channels. It was only by standing back a little distance that one could see that these channels, or most of them, converged on a single point and would ultimately unite. The common sense of the average citizen told him that "armed neutrality" was merely a half-way house and not a permanent refuge. He could see from the moment of Count Bernstorff's dismissal that the changes favored war. He looked forward to the prospect without enthusiasm, but with resignation. He knew that when the inevitable came it would be in spite of the President's most patient efforts to avert it. . . . The Zimmermann disclosures came just at the right moment to precipitate the hardening conviction that Germany was an international mischief-maker, a pest that had to be made an end of, and that even in the Americas there could be no security until chastisement had induced a radical change in her temper and ambitions. . . .

[W]hat was stirring . . . was . . . the perception, incredible at first, then admitted, then passing through various stages of doubt or hazy belief, and finally crystallizing into a pretty firm persuasion, that Germany under her present rulers, in her present spirit, was like some hideous scourge of old, some immensely multiplied Black Death pestilence, and that in the face of it all peoples and Governments ought to unite on instant measures of sanitation. We in Great Britain waked to this conclusion some time ago. But it was only after much questioning and turmoil of spirit that Americans, especially in the Middle West, where the Germans have formed a large, industrious, kindly and stable element of the population, could be induced to accept it. Nothing but the brutal argument of the facts could have forced them to revise their old conceptions of the Germans of Germany or to grasp the simple truism that they have transformed themselves into the enemies of mankind. . . .

What I seem to have witnessed in the past month or two is the steady approximation of the American point of view to the European point of view. Americans realize at last that Prussia is not as other States and that Prussianism is a disease that will infect the whole universe unless it is stamped out. They no longer therefore talk peace or think it. They understand that if the world is ever to be remodeled on a saner and safer plan Hohenzollernism and all it connotes must be destroyed; and that only when the Germans are convinced that militarism does not pay and that Prussianism is synonymous with disaster and humiliattion will they be cured of that "will to power" which has penetrated their whole attitude towards life and morals and the scheme of international relations; and that they will be cured of that cancer of the mind and heart by one thing and one thing only—unmistakable defeat. Politically the United States and the Allies in the prosecution of this war may remain separate until events, as they assuredly will, oblige them to make common cause at every point. But in sentiment, in objectives, in faith, in agreement as to what it fundamentally is that has to be done, they are one already. The President added a golden page to the literature of Liberty when he framed his address to Congress summoning it to war. There was not a line or a sug-

gestion in it that all the Allied Governments and peoples would
not enthusiastically endorse.

12   *For Freedom and Democracy*

The North American Review, *a conservative journal, summarizes the
ideological arguments utilized broadly to justify the American entrance
into World War I. These arguments appeared also in the liberal President Wilson's war message of April 2, 1917. The decision for war required massive rearmament but also pointed toward an internationalist
foreign policy.*

The issue is in doubt no longer. We know now, if we have
not known before, what this war is. It is the last of the great
battles for Freedom and Democracy. America fought the first a
century and forty years ago. France followed through seas of
blood and tears. But lately the Great Charter has passed in its
entirety from the barons to the people of England. Japan has
ceased to be a monarchy except in name. China as a Republic
defies the power of might. Portugal, freed by a bloodless revolution, stands with the Allies. Personal government has disappeared forever from every part of the Western hemisphere. And
now Russia, autocracy of autocracies, casts off the yoke and takes
her place in the sun of civilization. Can anyone doubt that the
beginning of the end of absolutism is at hand; that the thrones
of Hapsburgs and Mahomeds are crumbling; that the whole clan
Hohenzollern, no less of Greece and Bulgaria than of Prussia, is
doomed beyond recall; that liberty for the patient German people
is as certain as freedom for downtrodden Hungary, for despoiled
Servia and for bleeding Armenia?

So mighty a change cannot be wrought in a month or likely in
a year—and not at all unless and until the rulers of Central

SOURCE. "For Freedom and Democracy," *North American Review* (1917), **205**:
481–489.

Europe shall yield to a world of freemen. Wholly aside, then, from the injuries and insults which America has endured at the hands of the War Lord and which she is expected to advance as technical grounds for action, does not America's higher duty, her greater opportunity, lie along the path of the shot heard 'round the world? Are we to permit others to finish the glorious work which we began, according to even the infidel Allen, in the name of Almighty God? Shall we renounce our own professed ideals so completely that, at the end of the war, we may not deny as a matter of fitness and right, the transshipment of Liberty Enlightening the World from the harbor of New York to that of Hong Kong or Vladivostock? Must even China be allowed to forge ahead of America in defense of democracy?

We are for war; of course, we are; and for reasons good and plenty, to wit:

1. Because we have reached and passed the limit of for-bearance in trying to maintain amicable relations with a bar-baric brute who has presumed so far upon our good intent as to treat our most conciliatory and helpful suggestions with glar-ing contempt, who has incited all manner of treasonable activities and damnable outrages within our borders, had gloated over his avowed assassination of our innocent and harmless citizens of both sexes and all ages upon the high seas and has missed no opportunity to deceive, to sneer at and to lie to our constituted authorities; because to conserve our own self-respect we are driven finally to the point where we must fight or forfeit the decent opinion of all mankind; because we cannot even seem to condone the breaking of treaties, the burning of villages to no purpose except to deprive the poor and helpless of shelter essential to mere existence, the enslavement of men who alone could save their families from destitution and death from starvation, the violating of women and young girls, the bayonetting of little children, the approved indiscriminate slaughter by the unspeakable Turks of thousands of helpless Christians in Armenia, and God only knows what else and what more that has stamped the Hun for more than one generation to come as the sublimated hero of the shambles of humanity; because, in a word, we cannot acknowledge the supremacy of might and frightfulness over

right and righteousness without denying our faith in the living God.

2. Because we owe it to our forefathers who founded the Republic and to our fathers who saved the Union to prove ourselves not merely worthy of the happiness which flows from prosperity but eager and fearless in support of free life and full liberty the world over, to the end that the noble example set by them may not be degraded in gluttonous realization by us; because as a practical matter if spies and traitors infest our land now is the time to smoke them out; if a few scattering undersea waifs can break down our defenses and damage our cities, let them do their utmost that we may discover what might be anticipated from a fleet and prepare accordingly; if our navy is lopsided and deficient, our provision for a defensive army unfulfilled and unrealizable, our stores of ammunition insufficient, our airmachines and submarines but samples, today when only negligible harm can come to us is the day to acquaint ourselves with the facts; and if, as we are told, so many of us are pro-this or pro-that and so many more are putting self above patriotism and so many more should be feeding off our own fat instead of mulcting lean Chautauquans, then what we need is a test—a test of body, of mind and of spirit—a trying-out by fire while yet there is time to make America fit for any real emergency; yes, and able, through universal training, to obviate the necessity of universal service; because simply and finally, in such a case, war is curative, not destructive, a blessing, not a curse.

3. Because our going into the great conflict at this psychological moment would not only complete the ring of democracies around the doomed autocracy and so render the ultimate result certain to the dullest and the blindest, but also from that very fact would infect all Germany, all Austria and all Hungary with the new spirit of Russia, and so by surely shortening and perhaps quickly ending the war would save millions of precious finer perceptions as a being altogether worthy of our worshipful lives, certain else to be sacrificed to no purpose other than impoverishment of the human race for centuries to come.

13   *Norman Thomas et al.*
The Religion of Free Men

*The man who later became the revered leader of the American Social-
ist Party joined with a group of other young men to state the case for
conscientious objection to war on grounds of religion.*

SIR. As conscientious objectors we turn to your journal because more powerfully than any other it has expressed in subtle
analysis our abiding faith in humane wisdom. You have never
countenanced the evil doctrine of the brute coercion of the
human will. You have preached and practised the virtue of
tolerance, the kind of tolerance for the lack of which the state
grows mechanized and conscienceless.

You know something of the machinery of fair play. You
understand the tyranny of sham shibboleths. You appreciate
the menace of military psychology. We appeal to you, strategic-
ally situated as you are, to assist the cause of the conscientious
objectors. We beg you to note the following facts:

In the evolution of the human mind we discover a gradually
widening hiatus between physical competence and intellectual
moral competence. So deeply imbedded in our life values is this
distinction that we feel rather ashamed of being too expert
physically. The man of blood and iron does not appeal to our
finer perceptions as a being altogether worthy of our worshipful
attention. (The God whom we worship is neither a jingo nor
a militarist.) But Voltaire—he of the skinny shanks and the
anaemic face—what exuberant pride wells up in the greatest
and in the least of us at the sound of that marvelous name! And

SOURCE. Norman Thomas et al., "The Religion of Free Men," *New Republic*
(May 26, 1917), 109–111.

soft-spoken Jesus—what fitting tribute can the reeling world lay at the feet of him who died that good will and loving kindness might assuage the hearts of inimical men.

The complexity and richness of life have permitted, and increasingly so, the more or less free play of *all modes* of energy. There are many men best adapted by training and temperament to the performance of physical acts of heroism; there are some men more naturally suited to the performance of intellectual deeds of courage, while yet some others shine in deeds of moral bravery. Why sanction the inhuman device of forcing all manner of men into the narrowly specific kind of devotion for which so many of them are hopelessly unfit? Tolerance arises from the existence of varying types of doers all willing to respect one another's special competence. It is not too extreme to assert that in war time (as in peace time) some of the most heroic deeds are performed by those who do not (and, if called upon, would not) take up arms in defense of the cause. There are other forms of bravery than the purely military one. Let us be reasonable.

The one ineradicable fact which no amount of official intimidation can pulverize out of existence is that there is a type of man to whom (military) participation in war is tantamount to committing murder. He cannot, he will not, commit murder. There is no human power on God's earth that can coerce him into committing (what he knows to be) the act of murder. You may call him sentimentalist, fool, slacker, mollycoddle, woman—anything "disreputable" you please. But there he is, a tremendous fact. Shall he be maltreated for his scruples? Or shall he be respected (as his deriders are) for his conscientiousness? We cannot leave so momentous an issue to chance or to the cold machinery of administration. Men of sensitive insight must help prepare a social setting within America sufficiently hospitable to all conscientious objectors.

It is good to remind ourselves of our instinctive respect for conscientious objectors. When a man is called to serve on a jury empaneled in a murder case he may be honorably excused from duty if he has conscientious objections to the death penalty. When we think sanely we are not averse to honoring the man of conscience provided he be an active friend of mankind and not a mere ease-taker. The test of manhood lies in service; *not* in one particular kind of service (suitable to one particular type of mind and body), but genuine service genuinely rendered to humanity.

Hence the philosophic value of tolerance. To keep alive genuine tolerance in war time is the greatest single achievement to which rationalists can dedicate themselves. America is caught in this insidious entanglement; obsessed with the tradition—the mere outward form and symbol—of liberty-of-conscience, she has failed to realize the living need of a real grant and a substantial practice of our vaunted freedom-of-conscience. It is not the tradition we lack; only a vital *belief* in that tradition.

In times of precarious peace, when the social classes wage an almost relentless warfare and the daily grind of poverty and distress lays armies of the proletariat low, life for the disadvantaged groups is made more or less livable only by the thought that between them and their official superiors certain constitutional and humane guarantees of tolerance exist as safeguards of mutual understanding. There is room for difference of opinion. There is a breathing space for discussion. How desperate must the social situation have become if large numbers of conscientious and law-abiding citizens have begun to feel an appalling sense of uneasiness in the presence of huge, inscrutable forces, far beyond their power of control or sympathetic understanding. Why this amazing disquietude? The answer is simple and straightforward. There is no longer the sense—so natural and dear to free men—of being able to appeal from manifestly unfair decisions. Too many subordinate officials are being vested with a tremendous authority over impotent human beings. The situation is complicated and made more sinister by the suspicion that many of the powerful gentlemen who in the days of ampler opportunity for social service and social justice failed most lamentably to respond to the public's needs are now the unchallenged controllers of the social destiny. What we must not overlook in this perilous situation is this disquieting fact: an excess of power permits certain antisocial men to wield with utter unscrupulousness the whole machinery of antihumanism, of which by the sheer accident of circumstance they happen to be gaining possession at this critical time.

Then consider this: sooner or later war must cease. The tremendous enterprise of recreating out of bloody chaos some new, reinspired internationalism will be the order of the day.

Who is better fitted for that reconstructive task than those humanists now in imminent danger of being bullied out of existence because their visions and their faiths extend beyond the time of bloody chaos? It would be folly for a groping democracy to permit the degradation, the torture, and the slow innihilation of conscientious citizens. Whose duty shall it be to bring into permanent realization those humanist values (for which all men in their saner moments proudly contend) in behalf of which our war for democracy is said to be waged? If the reigning editorial intolerance, directed and sanctioned by official autocrats, is permitted to assassinate the greater promises held in trust by the workers for a world democracy, the outlook for a greater humanity is indeed mournful. Whom can we in this period of panic and pain rely upon? Humanitarians, workers in the social service, child welfare devotees, Tolstoians, radical educators—these constitute the vanguard of a revised and spiritually humanized world state. If civilization were to plan the utter wreckage of its most precious (because most consecrated) values, it could do no better than empower the mechanized state with the authority to brutalize and degrade all its visionaries.

Hasn't our evolving democracy any use for the student, the reflective man, the lonely thinker, the gentle philosopher, the socialist, the lover of Jesus, the vision-haunted educator, the pity-wracked lover of the human kind? Isn't sheer humanity itself a marvellous force for good? Is there no world recompense in having nurtured, honored, and immortalized Ralph Emerson, Henry Thoreau, Leo Tolstoi, Bertrand Russell, Norman Angell, and Romain Rolland? Is there no duty the conscientious thinker owes to the unborn world, the finer world of tomorrow, regenerated and recreated under the inspiration of the humanitarians? Can't we honestly respect the peculiar rights of those who have given their sincerest devotion to advocating the institution among men of that kind of livable régime by the very nature of which the present world calamity would have been rendered well-nigh unthinkable? Shall the dreamers of a true toleration of mankind be sacrificed because they have not yet been permitted to realize their dream?

We desire to contribute our intellectual and moral energies

to the creation of that humaner world in which conscience and tolerance and personality and philosophy will count as mightily as do their fierce negations now. . . .

We have not been schooled by life to play the military role. We have never found it necessary or desirable to inflict our philosophies with a rod. We have been able and willing to instruct a recreant mankind by force of example, by the persuasions of wisdom, by the practice of fair play. We have found our existence tolerable precisely because we have known how to substitute for the rigors of coercion the rigors of persuasion. We have no military competence. We possess only intellectual and moral competence. We would serve gladly, generously, high-heartedly—but we cannot serve except it be honestly, conscientiously, morally. . . .

14   *Randolph Bourne*
          The War and the Intellectuals

An embittered opponent of American intervention presents a jaundiced evaluation of the response of intellectuals to the decision for war, criticizing those who wished to convert the war into a struggle to make the world safe for democracy. Bourne died at the early age of thirty-two, but he became a hero of the "lost generation" during the twenties. His cult has experienced a revival in late years.

To those of us who still retain an irreconcilable animus against war, it has been a bitter experience to see the unanimity with which the American intellectuals have thrown their support to the use of war-technique in the crisis in which America found herself. Socialists, college professors, publicists, new-republicans, practitioners of literature, have vied with each other in con-

SOURCE. Randolph Bourne, "The War and the Intellectuals, *The Seven Arts* (1917), 2:133–136. Reprinted by permission of Harper & Row, Inc.

firming with their intellectual faith the collapse of neutrality and the riveting of the war-mind on a hundred million more of the world's people. And the intellectuals are not content with confirming our belligerent gesture. They are now complacently asserting that it was they who effectively willed it, against the hesitation and dim perceptions of the American democratic masses. A war made deliberately by the intellectuals! A calm moral verdict, arrived at after a penetrating study of inexorable facts! Sluggish masses, too remote from the world-conflict to be stirred, too lacking in intellect to perceive their danger! An alert intellectual class, saving the people in spite of themselves, biding their time with Fabian strategy until the nation could be moved into war without serious resistance! An intellectual class, gently guiding a nation through sheer force of ideas into what the other nations entered only through predatory craft or popular hysteria or militarist madness! A war free from any taint of self-seeking, a war that will secure the triumph of democracy and internationalize the world! This is the picture which the more self-conscious intellectuals have formed of themselves and which they are slowly impressing upon a population which is being led no man knows whither by an indubitably intellectualized President. And they are right in that the war certainly did not spring from either the ideals or the prejudices, from the national ambitions or hysterias, of the American people, however acquiescent the masses prove to be and however clearly the intellectuals prove their putative intuition.

Those intellectuals who have felt themselves totally out of sympathy with this drag toward war will seek some explanation for this joyful leadership. They will want to understand this willingness of the American intellect to open the sluices and flood us with the sewage of the war spirit. We cannot forget the virtuous horror and stupefaction which filled our college professors when they read the famous manifesto of their ninety-three German colleagues in defence of their war. To the American academic mind of 1914 defence of war was inconceivable. From Bernhardi it recoiled as from a blasphemy, little dreaming that two years later would find it creating its own cleanly reasons for imposing military service on the country and for talking of the rough rude currents of health and regeneration that war would send through the American body politic. They would have thought anyone mad who talked of shipping American men by the hundreds of thousands—conscripts—to die on the fields of France. Such a spiritual change seems catastrophic when we shoot our minds back to those days when neutrality was a proud thing. But the intellectual progress has been so gradual that the country retains little sense of the irony. The war sentiment, begun so gradually but so perseveringly by the preparedness advocates who came from the ranks of big business, caught hold of one after another of the intellectual groups. With the aid of Roosevelt the murmurs became a monotonous chant and finally a chorus so mighty that to be out of it was at first to be disreputable and finally almost obscene. And slowly a strident rant was worked up against Germany which compared very creditably with the German fulminations against the greedy power of England. The nerve of the war-feeling centred, of course, in the richer and older classes of the Atlantic seaboard and was keenest where there were French or English business and particularly social connections. The sentiment then spread over the country as a class-phenomenon, touching everywhere those upper-class elements in each section who identified themselves with this Eastern ruling group. It must never be forgotten that in every community it was the least liberal and least democratic elements among whom the preparedness and later the war sentiment was found. The farmers were apathetic, the small businessmen and workingmen are still apathetic towards the war. The election was a vote of confidence of these latter classes in a President who would keep the faith of neutrality. The intellectuals, in other words, have identified themselves with the least democratic forces in American life. They have assumed the leadership for war of those very classes whom the American democracy has been immemorially fighting. Only in a world where irony was dead could an intellectual class enter war at the head of such illiberal cohorts in the avowed cause of world-liberalism and world-democracy. No one is left to point out the undemocratic nature of this war-liberalism. In a time of faith skepticism is the most intolerable of all insults.

Our intellectual class might have been occupied during the last two years of war in studying and clarifying the ideals and

aspirations of the American democracy, in discovering a true
Americanism which would not have been merely nebulous but
might have federated the different ethnic groups and traditions.
They might have spent the time in endeavoring to clear the public
mind of the cant of war, to get rid of old mystical notions that
clog our thinking. We might have used the time for a great wave
of education, for setting our house in spiritual order. We could at
least have set the problem before ourselves. If our intellectuals
were going to lead the administration, they might conceivably
have tried to find some way of securing peace by making neutrality effective. They might have turned their intellectual energy
not to the problem of jockeying the nation into war but to the
problem of using our vast neutral power to attain democratic
ends for the rest of the world and ourselves without the use of
the malevolent technique of war. They might have failed. The
point is that they scarcely tried. The time was spent not in clari-
fication and education but in a mulling over of nebulous ideals
of democracy and liberalism and civilization, which had never
meant anything fruitful to those ruling classes who now so glibly
used them, and in giving free rein to the elementary instinct of
self-defence. The whole era has been spiritually wasted. The
outstanding feature has been not its Americanism but its intense
colonialism. The offence of our intellectuals was not so much
that they were colonial—for what could we expect of a nation
composed of so many national elements?—but that it was so one-
sidedly and partisanly colonial. The official reputable expression
of the intellectual class has been that of the English colonial.
Certain portions of it have been even more loyalist than the King,
more British even than Australia. Other colonial attitudes have
been vulgar. The colonialism of the other American stocks was
denied a hearing from the start. America might have been made
a meeting-ground for the different national attitudes. An intellectual class, cultural colonists of the different European nations,
might have threshed out the issues here as they could not be
threshed out in Europe. Instead of this, the English colonials in
university and press took command at the start, and we became
an intellectual Hungary where thought was subject to an effective process of Magyarization. The reputable opinion of the
American intellectuals became more and more either what could

be read pleasantly in London or what was written in an earnest effort to put Englishmen straight on their war-aims and war-technique. This Magyarization of thought produced as a counter-reaction a peculiarly offensive and inept German apologetic, and the two partisans divided the field between them. The great masses, the other ethnic groups, were inarticulate. American public opinion was almost as little prepared for war in 1917 as it was in 1914. . . .

We have had to watch, therefore, in this country the same process which so shocked us abroad—the coalescence of the intellectual classes in support of the military programme. In this country, indeed, the socialist intellectuals did not even have the grace of their German brothers to wait for the declaration of war before they broke for cover. And when they declared for war they showed how thin was the intellectual veneer of their socialism. For they called us in terms that might have emanated from any bourgeois journal to defend democracy and civilization, just as if it were not exactly against those very bourgeois democracies and capitalist civilizations that socialists had been fighting for decades. But so subtle is the spiritual chemistry of the "inside" that all this intellectual cohesion—herd-instinct become herd-intellect—which seemed abroad so hysterical and so servile comes to us here in highly rational terms. We go to war to save the world from subjugation! But the German intellectuals went to war to save their culture from barbarization! And the French went to war to save their beautiful France! And the English to save international honor! And Russia, most altruistic and self-sacrificing of all, to save a small State from destruction! Whence is our miraculous intuition of our moral spotlessness? Whence our confidence that history will not unravel huge economic and imperialist forces upon which our rationalizations float like bubbles? The Jew often marvels that his race along should have been chosen as the true people of the cosmic God. Are not our intellectuals equally fatuous when they tell us that our war of all wars is stainless and thrillingly achieving for good?

An intellectual class that was wholly rational would have called insistently for peace and not for war. For months the crying need has been for a negotiated peace in order to avoid the ruin of a deadlock. Would not the same amount of resolute states-

manship thrown into intervention have secured a peace that
would have been a subjugation for neither side? Was the terrific
bargaining power of a great neutral ever really used? Our war
followed, as all wars follow, a monstrous failure of diplomacy.
Shamefacedness should now be our intellectual's attitude, because the American play for peace was made so little more than
a polite play. The intellectuals have still to explain why, willing
as they now are to use force to continue the war to absolute exhaustion, they were not willing to use force to coerce the world
to a speedy peace. . . .

The results of war on the intellectual class are already apparent. Their thought becomes little more than a description
and justification of what is going on. They turn upon any rash
one who continues idly to speculate. Once the war is on, the
conviction spreads that individual thought is helpless, that the
only way one can count is as a cog in the great wheel. There is
no good holding back. We are told to dry our unnoticed and in-
effective tears and plunge into the great work. Not only is everyone forced into line but the new certitude becomes idealized.
It is a noble realism which opposes itself to futile obstruction
and the cowardly refusal to face facts. This realistic boast is so
loud and sonorous that one wonders whether realism is always a
stern and intelligent grappling with realities. May it not be
sometimes a mere surrender to the actual, an abdication of the
ideal through a sheer fatigue from intellectual suspense? The
pacifist is roundly scolded for refusing to face the facts and for
retiring into his own world of sentimental desire. But is the
realist, who refuses to challenge or criticise facts, entitled to any
more credit than that which comes from following the line of
least resistance? The realist thinks he at least can control events
by linking himself to the forces that are moving. Perhaps he
can. But, if it is a question of controlling war, it is difficult to
see how the child on the back of a mad elephant is to be any
more effective in stopping the beast than is the child who tries to
stop him from the ground. The ex-humanitarian, turned realist,
sneers at the snobbish neutrality, colossal conceit, crooked thinking, dazed sensibilities, of those who are still unable to find any
balm of consolation for this war. We manufacture consolations
here in America while there are probably not a dozen men fight-

ing in Europe who did not long ago give up every reason for their being there except that nobody knew how to get them away.

But the intellectuals whom the crisis has crystallized into an acceptance of war have put themselves into a terrifyingly strategic position. It is only on the craft, in the stream, they say, that one has any chance of controlling the current forces for liberal purposes. If we obstruct, we surrender all power for influence. If we responsibly approve, we then retain our power for guiding. We will be listened to as responsible thinkers, while those who obstructed the coming of war have committed intellectual suicide and shall be cast into outer darkness. Criticism by the ruling powers will only be accepted from those intellectuals who are in sympathy with the general tendency of the war. Well, it is true that they may guide, but if their stream leads to disaster and the frustration of national life, is their guiding any more than a preference whether they shall go over the right-hand or the left-hand side of the precipice? Meanwhile, however, there is comfort on board. Be with us, they call, or be negligible, irrelevant. Dissenters are already excommunicated. Irreconcilable radicals, wringing their hands among the debris, become the most despicable and impotent of men. There seems no choice for the intellectual but to join the mass of acceptance. But again the terrible dilemma arises—either support what is going on, in which case you count for nothing because you are swallowed in the mass and great incalculable forces bear you on, or remain aloof, passively resistant, in which case you count for nothing because you are outside the machinery of reality.

Is there no place left, then, for the intellectual who cannot yet crystallize, who does not dread suspense, and is not yet drugged with fatigue? The American intellectuals, in their preoccupation with reality, seem to have forgotten that the real enemy is War rather than imperial Germany. There is work to be done to prevent this war of ours from passing into popular mythology as a holy crusade. What shall we do with leaders who tell us that we go to war in moral spotlessness or who make "democracy" synonymous with a republican form of government? There is work to be done in still shouting that all the revolutionary by-products will not justify the war or make war anything else than the most noxious complex of all the evils that afflict men. There must be some to find no consolation whatever and some to sneer at those who buy the cheap emotion of sacrifice. There must be some irreconcilables left who will not even accept the war with walrus tears. There must be some to call unceasingly for peace and some to insist that the terms of settlement shall be not only liberal but democratic. There must be some intellectuals who are not willing to use the old discredited counters again and to support a peace which would leave all the old inflammable materials of armament lying about the world. There must still be opposition to any contemplated "liberal" world-order founded on military coalitions. The "irreconcilable" need not be disloyal. He need not even be "impossibilist." His apathy towards war should take the form of a heightened energy and enthusiasm for the education, the art, the interpretation that make for life in the midst of the world of death. The intellectual who retains his animus against war will push out more boldly than ever to make his case solid against it. The old ideals crumble; new ideals must be forged. His mind will continue to roam widely and ceaselessly. The thing he will fear most is premature crystallization. If the American intellectual class rivets itself to a "liberal" philosophy that perpetuates the old errors, there will then be need for "democrats" whose task will be to divide, confuse, disturb, keep the intellectual waters constantly in motion to prevent any such ice from ever forming.

PART TWO

Belligerency, 1917–1918

The right is more precious than peace, and we shall fight for the things we have always carried nearest to our hearts—for democracy, for the right of those who submit to authority to have a voice in their own Governments, for the rights and liberties of small nations, for a universal dominion of right by such a concert of free peoples as shall bring peace and safety to all nations and make the world itself at last free. PRESIDENT WOODROW WILSON, *April* 1917.

MOBILIZATION

15   *Louise Maunsell Field*
Sentimentalizing Over the Hun

This article is one of many hysterical efforts to stimulate hatred of the principal enemy as the United States went to war.

As a nation, we Americans are good-natured and somewhat sentimental. Moreover, our sentimentality is of a peculiarly amiable kind. Not only have we a strong taste for the pretty and the pleasant but even while vigorously doing our best to combat it we try to convince ourselves of the concealed prettiness and pleasantness of much that is essentially ugly. And never has this especial characteristic of ours been more markedly shown than during the period which has elapsed since it was acknowledged that we are at war with Germany. . . .

Now it would be difficult if not impossible to denounce the German Government unjustly or to accuse it of any crime of which it is not guilty, there being no crime known to history which it has not committed. But when we talk about it as though it were something entirely apart and different from the German people we make a mistake which is not only foolish but positively dangerous. For if it is a perilous thing to underestimate one's opponent physically, it is at least equally hazardous

SOURCE. Louise Maunsell Field, "Sentimentalizing Over the Hun," *Forum* (1917), **58**: 307–312.

to overestimate him morally. And this is precisely what we are doing when we sentimentalize over the poor deluded, naturally sweet-tempered and generally angelic Hun and weep about the way his Government forces him to do things entirely out of keeping with his kindly disposition.

That the Imperial German Government can lie with a fluency and persistency which would bring a blush of shame to the cheek of Ananias is a manifest and undeniable fact. But what is very far from being a manifest fact is that the utterly inhuman way in which Germany has carried on this war, the gospel of "frightfulness" it has proclaimed and practiced, is to any extent uncongenial to the temper of the German people. On the contrary, practically every particle of evidence indicates that it suits them to perfection.

It did not shock the German people to hear a solemn treaty comtemptuously described as "a scrap of paper." Honor is to them, it would seem, something which has to do with an officer's right to thrust civilians off the sidewalk and not with the keeping of a plighted word. The German Chancellor knew very well that he ran no risk of jarring against his people's sense of national probity; it is impossible to jar against that which does not exist.

And when the plighted word had been broken, and broken in a manner which caused the whole civilized world to cry out in horror and indignation, where was the protesting voice of the German people? While the German soldiers not merely obeyed orders—that might be forgiven them, though it is doubtful whether any other soldiers on earth would have obeyed such orders, with the possible exception of the Turks—but obeyed them joyfully. To shoot unarmed and wounded prisoners is not only contrary to the laws of war, it is contrary to every decent instinct of ordinary human nature. But German soldiers not only shot wounded prisoners under such direct orders as this, issued by General Stenger: "From and after today no more prisoners are to be taken. All prisoners, whether wounded or not are to be killed"; they did it with pleasure and such delightful additions as beating or kicking their heads to a pulp. In an extract from the notebook of a German noncommissioned officer we read: "The Captain called us round him and said: 'In the fort we are going to take there will probably be English soldiers. But I don't wish to see any English prisoners with my company.' A general Bravo! of approval was the answer." A general Bravo! of approval was the answer! Surely comment is superfluous.

But, it may be objected, the German army is not the German people. Then what, pray, are the officers and men of the German army? Do they belong to a race apart? Are they not the sons of German parents, the husbands of German women, the fathers of German children, the heads of German families? It is a fact whose significance we are only now beginning to appreciate that the number of German children who commit suicide is so large. . . .

It is time that we here in the United States looked the truth squarely in the face, recognizing that we have to fight a united nation, not one divided into a government entirely vicious, misleading a people possessed of the innocence, the intelligence and the docility of sheep. We do not intend to sing hymns of hate or indulge in any other equally childish performances. But it is time we stopped sentimentalizing over the Hun, and realize that if it were repugnant instead of congenial to him to perform such barbarous cruelties that beside his deeds those of the Huns of old appear white and shining, almost meritorious, no government or earth could force him to be guilty of them. . . . We are at war, not with a mere government, but with a nation of moral perverts, a nation which exults in torture, admires murder, and has no faintest conception of the meaning of the word honor. There are of course exceptions; here and there in the notebooks of German soldiers we find comments such as this: "This method of making war is absolutely barbarous. I wonder how we can have the face to rail at the conduct of the Russians when we are behaving much worse in France; at every opportunity, on one pretext or another, we pillage and burn. But God is just and sees everything. His mills grind slowly, but they 'grind exceeding small.' " A nation, however, must be judged by the bulk of its people, not by the exceptions. We have learned to call the German soldier or sailor "the Hun"; but the soldier and sailor are not a race apart. The individual Hun comes from a nation of Huns. . . .

We have, very many of us, taken our ideas of the German character and temperament from the tales of the Brothers Grimm and the poems of Heine—who, by the way, lived in France!—but we must disabuse our minds of such mistaken impressions, stop sentimentalizing, and look upon the German people as what they are: that people whose barbarity has earned for them a nickname, the name of greatest infamy that men have been able to remember or to conceive—the Huns.

16   *Lee Simonson*
          Mobilizing the Billboards

The author calls for effective use of artistic talent in order to provide posters and billboards that properly dramatized the requirements of the war.

Nothing could have been more irrelevant to the man in the street than our first recruiting posters. For the man in the street, whether he signed a recruit's oath, bought a liberty bond, or subscribed to the Red Cross, saw the shark's-snout of a submarine, Rheims ablaze, leprous shell craters, No Man's Land swallowing its dead. His composite picture of the war, set flaming and thundering by newspaper headlines, had become as definitely a drama of good and evil as any medieval vision of the plains of purgatory and the tiers of hell. What he found on the billboards, as a rule, was nothing more than the star-spangled chorus of a roof garden.

Columbia and Uncle Sam paraded in new bunting. Soldiers in new uniforms stood at attention while the flag was waved and the patriotic finale was sung. Such sailors as appeared were the same blond youths who had demonstrated the neat fit of Arrow

SOURCE. Lee Simonson, "Mobilizing the Billboards," *New Republic* (November 10, 1917), 41–43.

brand collars in the street cars. Having suffered a sea change, they appeared bare-necked in white sailor blouses. Whatever tag these posters bore, they conveyed nothing but the puerile assurance that it is splendid to wear a uniform. Uncle Sam occasionally lost his temper and pointed an angry finger. At times Columbia slept, pillowed in a wicker chair presumably on a hotel veranda. The poster read, "America, wake up!" And we were asked to assume that Columbia, once awakened, would suddenly become the goddess of national energy.

So complete a failure to touch popular imagination is made possible because publicity committees, national or local, have failed to realize the qualities essential to posters if they are to become effective substitutes for heralds' banners or towncriers' bells. A poster is an advertisement made beautiful in order to be more convincing, a mural decoration that successfully harangues the crowd. Its beauty is a sudden and unexpected sim-plicity, violent juxtaposition of silhouettes, vivid patterns of light and shade that hold the eye spellbound at fifty feet, sono-rous clashes of color that sound above all the other noises of the street with the insistence of trumpets or chimes. A poster's meaning should be latent in every image it uses so that, at its first words, they become militant symbols. And for that reason a poster designer's understanding of human psychology must equal his skill as a designer, for his problem is always twofold: to find the basic appeal of whatever cause he is advocating and, once that is determined, to dramatize it widely against an ap-propriate background. Without graphic gifts he will produce nothing more potent than an ugly advertisement. Without a genuine sense of what advertising means he will create deco-rations, beautiful but irrelevant.

The only artists in America equipped to produce the posters we need are a group of younger American designers who for the past three or four years have succeeded in beautifying some of our advertisements. Mr. Treidler and Mr. Britton are two of this group, and their posters were the first effective aid the nation's billboard campaign has had. Analyze Mr. Treidler's poster for the Liberty Loan. Its color scheme, Liberty, violently sketched in black and gold against a space of intensely blue sky, carried like a surging note from any window as far as the top of any passing bus. Instantly legible were the words "Liberty Loan" and a huge question mark poised in the sky. Mr. Treidler challenged response by allowing a symbol of doubt to dominate his whole design. At first glance the poster made plain that the success of the Liberty Loan was at stake. The words "Have you bought your bond?" explained the issue. With nothing more said, the case for the loan was unequivocably directed at every passersby, staged spaciously and with a touch of beauty. . . .

We may be reluctant to advertise war measures systematically, remembering "the deceptive clamor on the billboards which habitually disfigures the scenery, covers fences, plasters the city, blinks and winks through the night." But the fact remains that a nation is forced to advertise its needs in order to win recruits, just as a manufacturer is forced to advertise his promises in order to gain purchasers. What we advertise in time of peace are the trivial alternatives of using one brand of soup, toothpaste or hosiery rather than another. When the choice is not irrevocable, catch-words, bluff and buncombe, spectacular display of letters nine feet high or a thousand lamps flashing in unison may entice a buyer. But in advertising the fundamental alternatives of famine or plenty, life or death, we are forced to use the more inevitable eloquence of poetry and imagination by which any creed is communicated to a people. In pretending that the war is not being advertised, we shall merely continue to advertise it unintelligently, with the random jingoism and spontaneous puerility of our first advertisements for recruits. But the billboards can be successfully mobilized, if our administrators possess sufficient imagination to make these demands tangible, capable of being experienced by the public as a whole.

Although our poster designers fail to create new symbols, they may nevertheless reanimate old ones, blazon cities with insistent heraldry, devise weird legends for our hopes, create visions which will make the elation of volunteering, subscribing or dieting as emphatic as the elation of gaining a fine view from the crest of a hill. Such posters are needed to voice their summons in every other street—a summons that can sound as appropriately from walls and fences as from the throats of trumpets or the bellies of drums.

17   *Florence Woolston*
                Billy and the World War

*The mobilization touched the lives of nearly all Americans, even in-
cluding children, as the author indicates in her sensitive portrayal of
"Billy."*

Billy, my nephew, is twelve years old. With the possible exception of the beef profiteers and a few superpatriots to whom
life has been a prolonged Fourth of July oration, no one has
got quite so much fun out of the war as Billy and his inseparable
companions, Fritters, George and Bean-Pole Ross.

Clad in the khaki uniform of the Boy Scouts, with United
War Campaign, Red Cross, War Saving, first, second, third and
fourth Liberty Loan buttons, small American flags and service
pins spread across their chests, they have lived the war from
morning until night. I did not understand Billy's passionate
allegiance to the Scout uniform until I discovered the great
game of hailing automobiles bearing the sign, "Men in Uniform
Welcome." Billy has never been willing to accompany his family
on automobile rides but the pleasure of this boulevard game
has been never ending.

They call the suburb in which Billy lives one hundred per
cent patriotic. Everybody is in war work. Even the children
under five years have an organization known as the Khaki Babes.
These infants in uniform assemble, kindergarten fashion and
solemnly snip for the Red Cross. Billy's crowd is indefatigable
in its labors. With the other Scouts, the boys usher at meetings,
assist in parades, deliver bundles and run errands. They are
tireless collectors of nutshells, peach pits and tinsel paper. As
Victory Boys they are pledged to earn five dollars for the United

SOURCE. Florence Woolston, "Billy and the World War," *New Republic*
(January 25, 1919), 369–371.

War Workers. Since most of them expect to do this shovelling snow they are praying for a severe winter.

One bit of voluntary war work was carried on through the periods of the gasolineless Sundays when the four boys took positions on Commonwealth Avenue in such a way as to obstruct passing vehicles. If a car did not carry a doctor's or military sign, they threw pebbles and yelled "O you Slacker!" It was exciting work because guilty drivers put on full speed ahead and Billy admitted that he was almost run over, but he added that the cause was worth it.

In my school days history was a rather dull subject. Perhaps this was not a necessity but our teachers made it a certainty. Looking back, I seem to recall chiefly lists of battles, dates, kings and presidents. Wars were as unreal as pictorial combats with painted soldiers and stationary warships. Even the Civil War belonged to historical fiction. Once a year, on the 30th of May, a veteran in navy blue came to school and in a quavering voice told stories of his war days. Thrilling as they might have been, they always seemed to lack reality; they belonged with the monuments and historical tablets that flourish around Boston. As for current events, I think they were taboo in our school. We may have connected ourselves with politics by seeing an occasional torchlight parade but it is my impression that we never discussed anything that happened after 1865.

It is not so with Billy. Modern history is unfolding to him as a great drama. Kings and tsars and presidents are live human beings. War has nothing to do with books. It is a perpetual moving picture with reels furnished twice a day by the newspapers. Geography has also come out of the textbook. In our day we recited boundaries, principal cities, rivers, mountains and exports. Germany was a big yellow patch on the map, France was pink, Russia purple, Italy green and the British Isles were blue. It did not occur to us that they were peopled by human beings like ourselves. When we read stories of other lands, we did not connect Dutch, Italian, French and Russian children with the colored patches on the map.

To Billy and his chums geography is in the making. They know what boundaries mean; they pore over war maps and glibly recite the positions of the Allied troops. Billy has a

familiarity with principal cities, rivers and towns that never
could have been learned in lesson form. The war has created
a new cosmopolitanism. The children of Billy's generation will
never have the provincial idea that Boston is the centre of the
world. They will see the universe as a great circle, perhaps, but
all the Allies will occupy the centre.

I must confess, however, that Billy, Fritters, George and Bean-
Pole Ross have a rather vague idea of what the war is about,
but then so do others with more years to their credit. I asked
Billy what caused the war originally, and he replied in a rather
large and lofty way, "You see, the French took Alsace and Lor-
raine away from the Germans a long time ago and Germany
wanted it back. She thought it would be nice to get hold of
Paris, too, and conquer the French people, then they would
have to pay taxes and indemnities to support Germany. So they
started to march to Paris and then all the other countries decided to stop them."

When I compare the anemic stereopticon travel talks of my
school days with Billy's moving picture shows, I have the sense
of a cheated childhood. We had nothing in our young lives like
Crashing Through to Berlin, The Hounds of Hunland, Wolves
of Kultur and the Brass Bullet. Billy's mental images have been
built by such pictures as these with the additional and more educational films of the Committee on Public Information and the
Pathé weekly where actual battle scenes, aeroplane conflicts and
real naval encounters are portrayed.

In the matter of books, too, Billy has had high revel. I sowed
a few wild oats with Oliver Optic and Horatio Alger wherein
poor lads were conducted from prairie huts to the Executive
mansion. Of course we had Scott and Cooper to make medieval
times an Indian days vivid. But think of reading Over the Top
and going to shake hands with the author, a live, red-blooded
officer in the army! Billy revels in Private Peat, Hunting the
Hun, Out of the Jaws of Hunland, From Base Ball to Boches,
and With the Flying Corps. I'm afraid he will never have a
Walter Scott period and I am sure it will be years before con-
templative literature can hold his attention.

Of course, the war has given us all an enlarged vocabulary.

Billy calls his school "the trench"; he and Fritters go "over the top," "carry on," play in dug-outs, move in units, carry kits, eat mess and have elaborate systems of wig-wagging and passwords. When he is unsuccessful in a parental encounter, Billy throws up his hands and cries "I surrender!" Hun, Boche and Bolshevik are terms of terrible opprobrium. There was a bloody fist fight at recess recently, when Henry Earl was called "O you Kaiser!" The mere suggestion of a German name brings forth expressions of loud disgust and none of the boys would use a toy made in Germany.

At present it is in fashion to collect war posters. Billy has a remarkable collection of Food, Red Cross, Marine, War Savings, Navy and United War Work Campaign posters. He has trudged miles and spent much ingenuity in getting them. His room is papered with them and it is a matter of deep regret that the family is unwilling to have the entire house so placarded. A thriving business goes on in poster trading and a steady stream of small boys passes the house carrying large rolls of posters. From Billy's room, after a visitation, come delighted exclamations, "Gee! what a bute!" "Say, I'll give you a Join the Gas Hounds for a Beat Back the Huns." "Fritters has two Teufelhunden and he's going to swap it for a Clear the Way and a Tell That to the Marines."

Billy came to me with an ethical problem connected with his poster campaign. "I've got," he declared, "five Joan of Arcs, three Must Children Starves, five Blot it Outs, a Britisher and a big Y. I can sell them and make lots of money. Would that be profiteering?" I thought it might be so considered by taxpayers. "Well," he demanded, "If I sell them and buy Thrift Stamps that would be profiteering to help the war, and that would be all right, wouldn't it?"

When a campaign is on, the boys find it hard to wait until the posters have done their work as propaganda. Sometimes a lucky boy gets a whole new set. Recently, there had been much buying and selling of addresses where posters may be obtained, five cents for a plain address, ten for a "guaranteed." I mailed a postal card for Billy addressed to the Secretary of the Navy which read, "Kindly send me a full set of your Marine and Navy posters. I will display them if you wish." Billy's collection numbers about two hundred but he knows boys who have a thousand posters. As evidence of his great delight in them, he made the following statement: "If the last comes to the last, and we couldn't get coal and we had to burn all the furniture, I'd give up one set of my duplicates, but only if the last comes to the last."

Billy is a kind-hearted lad with humane instincts toward all creatures except flies. He feels, however, that the Kaiser can neither claim the protection of the S.P.C.A. nor demand the consideration usually afforded a human being. He loves to tell what he would do to the Kaiser. It is a matter of bitter disappointment that Mr. Hohenzollern is in Holland instead of in Billy's hands. At breakfast he issues bulletins of carnage. Some days he plans simple tortures like beheading, skinning, hanging, burning. At other times he concocts a more elaborate scheme such as splitting open the Kaiser's arms and putting salt on the wound, cutting his legs off at the knee and hanging his feet around his neck, or gouging out his eyes. A favorite idea is that of inoculating him with all the diseases of the world or to starve him for months and then eat a big Thanksgiving dinner in his presence.

Billy has had a full course in atrocities and is keen for reprisals. He longs to fly with an aviation unit, dropping bombs on Berlin, he aches to destroy a few cathedrals and palaces, burn all the German villages and poison the reservoirs. His description of what he would do to the Huns makes the Allied armistice sound like a presentation speech with a bunch of laurel.

There is a marked absence of patriotic sentiment with Billy and his chums. To them patriotism is action; they do not enjoy talking about it. When a Liberty Loan orator gushes about the starry banner, they roll their eyes expressively and murmur "Cut it out." Of course, some of this is the self-conscious stoicism of the small boy. But there is a matter of fact attitude toward suffering and pain which is new and due to familiarity with the idea. Boys discuss the kinds of wounds, operations and war accidents as a group of medical students might refer to a clinic.

Death seems to give them no sense of mystery and awe. "Gee! a thousand killed today," "That Ace has got his," "Say, John Bowers was gassed and he's gone now." They look over the casualty lists as grown-ups might read lists of guests at a reception. It may be because youth cannot understand the tragedy and heartache back of the golden stars on the service flags, but I think it goes deeper than that. These boys have a sense of courage and gallantry that makes the risking of life an everyday affair. Self-sacrifice is not a matter of poems and sermons and history, it is the daily news. Billy's attitude is that going to war is part of the game; when you're a little boy you have to go to school; when you're older, you draw your number and are called to camp—it's all in a day's work.

The weakest spot in Billy's war programme is food conservation. He does not readily respond to the sacrifice of sugar. At the first news of peace he brightened up with the query, "Now can we have frosting again and will chocolate sundaes be ten cents?" He did not come up to the plan of voluntary rationing at all; he was willing to do any amount of war work, he said, but he must have something to do it on. His mother told a pitiful tale of hungry boys in Belgium and what a small sacrifice on his part would do for them. Billy listened patiently, but unmoved. "Don't you care at all how dreadfully they need food?" she asked. "I'm sorry for them, Mother, of course," he replied, "But, Gee! that's their tough luck."

At five o'clock on the morning of November 11th when the bells and whistles were sounding news of the armistice Billy stole out to meet Fritters, George and Bean-Pole Ross. He left a note pinned to his pillow, "Will be back by and by. Can't help being patriotic and I must make a noise."

18 Walter S. Gifford
A National Picture Puzzle

This comment by the Director of the Council of National Defense summarizes the problems of mobilization as they seemed to present themselves at the outset of belligerency. The article reflects both the naïvité and the vitality of the American people at the time. It also reflects the mentality of progressive businessmen and the popular pragmatism so pervasive during that period.

I am asked "What does it mean to say that the Council of National Defense is mobilizing the resources of this nation?"

It means, as I see it, order. It means that everything should proceed in orderly fashion rather than in confused chaotic fashion. It means a definite channel for the definite things to be accomplished. It means responsible people responsible for important matters, and the avoidance of duplication of effort and division of responsibility.

The whole problem is like a picture puzzle: you have to catch each piece up and put it into the right place. It's like a picture puzzle except that the pieces never have been put together and some pieces don't belong and you have no box to throw them into when they get mixed or you get tired! It is simple enough, however, if you see that the piece you have in view will fit, but you must have in mind some scheme. You can't build blindly.

This leads to one of the reasons why, very often, people who want to help cannot be used. But because they don't understand organization often they don't understand why they can't be used. That's one of the difficult things. There are many patriotic, enthusiastic people who have ideas, often pet ideas, and it is necessary frequently to tell them that the particular way they have organized their idea, or the particular field, is

SOURCE. Walter S. Gifford, "A National Picture Puzzle," *Independent* (1917), 90:237.

such that it doesn't fit into the organization. It's very hard to say so, usually, because of the spirit that prompts the effort, but someone has to say so in order to get the job done right.

The situation before us is this: our problem isn't, in the first instance, one that demands hasty, hysterical action. Fortunately in this country we have concerns that have been making munitions. The question of supplying men to be raised within a year for the Army and Navy should not be a difficult one, but merely one of good sense business organization. The problem of supplying the civilian population and their needs will be complicated only by the condition of the harvests and by causes that might have occurred had there been no war—weather, for instance, and of course by the absence of men and by the demands of our Allies and their civilian populations. Let it be understood, in other words, that there are no more people to feed and clothe in this country than there were before war broke out and therefore the problem only becomes serious insofar as it is necessary for us to feed and clothe our Allies, which may mean some sort of restrictive measures here. Of course we might say that ultimately we shall take many million men away. If that should happen our problem would be made more serious, due to depletion of our man power, but such a situation is, at worst, many months off.

Our program at first should by all means be to maintain the normal economic and industrial conditions of the country as they are. No changes should be made in hours of labor, in the welfare of workers or in pay unless and until conditions have arisen which makes such changes imperative and necessary— clearly necessary. The important thing is for us to maintain with the least possible upset our present economic system. To this end the Government should buy its materials on some basis that will allow a fair profit to the producer; otherwise bankruptcy will result and a complete disruption of our economic system will occur.

I think Labor will sit tight and work, if it is treated fairly. If it is clearly understood that the producers are obtaining only a reasonable profit I think Labor will be willing to remain quietly at home in the factory and offer no objection to working under the conditions which obtained in peace time and even under conditions which have been changed due to absolute necessity on account of the war. For it will be remembered that other men are at the front fighting while these men are at home with their families, comfortable. It is plain, to look at the other side of the problem, that any scheme which requires Labor to endure more hardships than are necessary would certainly not be efficient and under no conditions would be justified. The only object in view must be to win the war and for everyone to endure sacrifices to the limit for this end. If these sacrifices are made unnecessarily great, looked at from the point of view of the good of the nation, they are wasteful and not useful in assisting to win the war. We must not work men twenty-four hours a day; do that and they break down and the nation suffers.

Our problem is a tremendous problem, yet it is a relatively simple problem when compared to what most people think it is. We have people who want to inventory the whole country and whole sections of the country. But what do we want such an inventory for? Let's stick to the problem we have before us and let every move that we make be a move toward the solution of the kind of things we have to solve. Let us drop other moves. Then the matter becomes simple in comparison with what it would be if we grabbed every idea and associated it with American defense. Let us apply a test to anything that anyone wants us to use. Let us inquire: does this actually help a particular plan of war that was given us to carry through? Will it help the Allies? Will it help the Navy? Will it help the Army? Will it help the civilian population? And, if so, is it necessary?

Of course all this is only the story of the way I see the situation. Conditions may be changed absolutely in six or eight months and many different measures may be necessary. But we must not undertake now things that may not be necessary for some months or years to come—that is an essential thing to remember.

We have the advantage of European experience. Much of this experience can be made use of in this country, but, on the other hand, much of it does not fit in.

Ours is a problem of itself. We must approach it, we must handle it, with that thought in mind.

19   *America's Food Problem*

This article, prepared by the United States Food Administration headed by Herbert C. Hoover, illustrates the government's efforts to shape popular attitudes and practices in respect to one critical national problem. It also illustrates the pervasive appeal to democracy as the reason for sacrifice.

"Our problem," says the Home Card of the Food Administration, now hanging in twelve million American kitchens, "is to feed our allies by sending them as much food as we can of the most concentrated nutritive value in the least shipping space. These foods are wheat, beef, pork, dairy products, and sugar. Our solution of this problem is to eat less of these, and more of other foods of which we have an abundance, and to waste less of all foods."

To quote Mr. Hoover, "We hold it in our power, and our power alone, to keep the wolf from the door of the world. This is a problem greater than war. It is a problem of humanity."

The United States holds the key to this problem. We have always been the greatest granary, food store, and butcher shop in the world, and our resources have by no means reached the limit of our development. Food, regular, good and sufficient for our mighty fighting armies—our own and our allies—for the working men and women behind the trench lines, for the old people, women and children, must be supplied if the war is to be won, and we can supply it.

WHY CONSERVATION IS NECESSARY

Millions of men in Europe have been withdrawn from farm and field to fight, and many thousands have been sent into

SOURCE. "America's Food Problem," *Independent* (1917), 92:572.

factories to equip the fighters with munitions of war. This means that less food is produced in the countries of our allies. Moreover, the hard work of war activities has meant an increased demand upon food supply. The decreased food production and increased food demand have made a yawning chasm in Europe which only America can bridge.

Now from the forecasted harvests of this country and Europe, and from our combined stocks of animals, we learn that we shall have to use the available supply with the utmost care and wisdom in order to have enough for all.

WHEAT IS NEEDED FIRST

France, Great Britain, Italy and Belgium need for their normal use nearly six million bushels of wheat more than they can produce. The Central Powers control the grain available in Russia, Bulgaria and Rumania, so that our allies cannot draw upon these supplies. Australia and India are practically cut off because of the long journey, the shortage in shipping and submarine danger. The South American crop was a failure, and the new harvest cannot reach Europe until next spring.

In short, the Allies need 577,000,000 bushels of wheat and we have a surplus of 208,000,000 bushels. Out of this surplus a certain amount must be kept for friendly neutrals. Therefore, if we continue to consume as much wheat as usual, there will be a deficit in round figures of 400,000,000 bushels.

HOW CAN AMERICA HELP?

Some of us have not understood why we must send wheat instead of corn, since corn is plentiful and of high food value. Why not keep our wheat and let our allies have corn? There are several good reasons:

1. Cornmeal cannot be shipped long distances without spoiling in transit.

2. Corn cannot be shipped in the grain because few mills in Europe except in Italy are equipped to grind it.

3. Cornmeal can best be used in home-baked breads, as corn bread is not suitable for bakery distribution. In France very little home baking is done, and most of the houses are not equipped for baking. In America, on the other hand, home baking is the rule.

Remember that our allies are already using as large a proportion of other cereals with wheat as is practicable with bakery bread. Their wheat is adulterated fourteen per cent in the milling. Before it can be made into bread, a further admixture of twenty per cent of other cereals is required—as high as fifty per cent allowed. Thus the minimum adulteration is thirty-four per cent. The Food Administration is asking Americans to do much less than the Allies are already doing. It is asking them to use twenty per cent of other cereals in place of that much wheat and to send to Europe the wheat thus released. This will only partly make up their shortage, but it will help.

OTHER FOODS NEEDED

Meat is another food especially needed that we must export in larger quantity. The people who are fighting and making war supplies need more meat that they would in peace times. But the reproduction of cattle, sheep and hogs has lessened by 33,000,000 in Europe and they have been compelled to "eat into the herd" to an alarming extent. Also an extra demand for wool and leather clothing for soldiers has meant a decrease of animals.

From the 1st of July, 1915, to the 30th of June, 1916, we exported more than 1,500,000,000 pounds of animal products and fats. We are selling faster than we can produce them. Of course this condition calls for increased production, but it also means that for the present conservation is of the gravest importance: to save out of what we have. Fats are fuel which fighters must have. We must send lard, bacon and other fats to our allies. To do this we shall have to reduce our own consumption. In many cases we use much more of these commodities than we need and waste them shockingly.

Another necessary food staple that our allies must have is sugar. They formerly got it from Russia, Germany, Austria and Java. Now they are dependent upon us and the sources which supply us.

One other aspect of food conservation as a war measure should be mentioned. Wars are paid for out of the people's pocket. If we wish to avoid financial troubles we ought to carry on this war to a great extent paying "as we go." If we reduce the waste and unwise use of food by only six cents a day for each person in our population we shall have saved more than two billion dollars a year.

EVERY AMERICAN MUST HELP

Each one of us wants to help, but sometimes we feel stunned by these huge sums and amounts. A million dollars, a million bushels! We gasp, "But how can I do anything? I am only one, and I have no millions to give or save." Then is the time to recall the old rime about the "little drops of water, little grains of sand." These vast amounts are composed of dollars, quarters, dimes, nickels, pennies; they are composed of shovelfuls, basketfuls, cupfuls, teaspoonfuls. Just remember that if each individual saves one pound of wheat flour a week and six cents' worth of meat, fats and sugar a day, it will mean enough to win through.

AUTOCRACY VERSUS SELF-GOVERNMENT

We are in this war and must do our share in winning it. One of our chief tasks is to supply food for our allies and their armies. We must decide how this is to be done. As time goes on it will get no easier to ship food and supply ourselves. We can meet the situation by force or by voluntary effort. The one way is autocracy; the other is self-government—democracy. It is the ideal, hope and aim of the Food Administration that our saving

and our organization for saving shall be voluntary and democratic. Democracy is the faith for which our men are dying in
France today. Every man, woman and child left here at home
must stand back of every soldier "over there" and help in the
daily service of conservation.

"AND A PULL ALL TOGETHER"

Every single person in this democracy has the opportunity of
the centuries to take part in the greatest adventure for democracy
ever known. Democracy is worth it. Your right to your own life,
to liberty, and to the pursuit of happiness is worth your service,
your cooperation, your devotion.

20   *Albert W. Atwood*
                         Mergeritis

*The war stimulated a surge of industrial concentration, inadvertantly
sponsored in great part by the federal government. This trend was in
opposition to the practice of "trustbusting" that prevailed before the
war. Rooseveltian Progressives found this development quite acceptable,
but it greatly alarmed Wilsonians who were forced to sponsor the re-
orientation.*

Never before has the civilized world been so committed as
now to a policy of giant mergers in industry, to concentration,
combination and consolidation. For the war has accelerated, has
indeed forced, a tendency that was already irresistible. We see
it not only in this country but in England, Canada, Japan and
Germany. Everywhere there are big units in industry—big busi-

SOURCE. Albert W. Atwood, "Mergeritis," *Saturday Evening Post* (July 13,
1918), 16, 38, 40, 43, 45. Copyright © by Albert W. Atwood. Reprinted by permission of Albert W. Atwood.

ness, if you will. Without it war on the present scale would be impossible.

It is curious how little we appreciate or are really interested in the extent to which this process has gone. Of course there are more important things to think about in these grave days, but the amalgamation process in industry, the continual forming of mergers, is not only a first-rate tool or instrument of war, it is the result of more or less blind economic forces that are sweeping us on, war or no war, to an unseen destiny. Nor does it lack a more immediate and human interest. Never is there any great upward movement in the stock market without mergers or rumors of mergers proving either an essential cause or effect of the speculative turmoil.

Business genius finds its expression largely in creating big units and big outputs. Of course it is not every banker or manufacturer whose ambition aspires to the high state of another J. Pierpont Morgan with his steel trust. But the careers of the most outstanding modern leaders of industry and finance in America, England and Germany are identified with the origination and management of vast business establishments. This is true not only of individuals but of families, groups, communities of interest or whatever form the leadership of capital and industry may take. We had or have Harriman, Hill, Morgan, the Rockefellers, Standard Oil, the Du Ponts, Ford, Schwab and a host of others. The story of mergers is the story of the ever-changing panorama of personalities in the great struggle for business success, eminence and dominance.

TRUSTBUSTING

It was only a few years ago that this country was engaged in a tremendous, though now almost forgotten, process of trustbusting. It was felt by most people that the merger movement had gone too far and had developed many evils. So the United States Supreme Court dissolved the Standard Oil Company, the American Tobacco Company and the Du Pont Powder Company. Other "trusts" were sued and their alleged sins much exposed in the lower courts. Even the intangible money trust was flayed up and down the land and investigated without end. The more conspicuous railroad mergers, like those achieved by Hill, Harriman and Mellon, were torn apart. The whole country was engaged in a crusade against monopoly.

But now the entire scenery has changed. We have a complete new set. The attitude, the feeling, the atmosphere have become different to the point of revolution. It has been due partly to the immediate needs of war, partly to a boundless growth in wealth and prosperity. To begin with, the trusts that were busted into many parts do not seem to have suffered at all, for each part has grown almost as big as the original trust. Stranger yet, numbers of previously small independents have grown so enormously that they now almost resemble the original trusts.

Instead of punishing companies for acting in concert the Government is now in some cases forcing them to unite, the most recent instance being the express companies. Only a few years ago the Government was busily breaking up single systems of railroads into their early component parts. Now it has put all the railroads in the country under one supreme control. The antitrust suits against the United States Steel Corporation and the American Sugar Refining Company have been quietly dropped, or at least suspended for the duration of the war, and the Supreme Court has just refused to dissolve the so-called shoe-machinery trust, declaring that the magnitude of the company was at once the cause and effect of efficiency.

Congress has just passed a law that makes it expressly legal for manufacturers to combine for export trade. The Sherman Anti-Trust Act, it is true, still stands upon the books and forbids domestic trusts. But every day the Government is actually compelling manufacturers to get together for the purpose of agreeing on prices, which was the specific crime most often punished under the Sherman Law of a few years ago. Hoover, the Food Administrator, urges milk distributors to combine in the interests of economy, though it seems but yesterday that the milk trust was anathema.

After seeking in vain for an independent organization capable of handling such a mammoth undertaking the Government was compelled to ask the United States Steel Corporation, the largest private industrial unit on earth, to construct and operate the new ordnance plant near Pittsburgh. Charles M. Schwab, head of a steel company big enough to be considered a trust by the standards of ten years ago, and John D. Ryan, head of the world's largest copper combination and perhaps the country's most ardent advocate and tireless worker in the interests of corporate cooperation, have been summoned by the Government to take charge of the manufacture of shipping and aircraft, respectively.

But it must not be supposed that the trust busting of a few years ago was a wholly futile and misdirected effort. The surgery was performed by a blunt, ill-chosen tool, but it was performed all the same. No longer do you find the captains of finance advocating and defending the old-fashioned trust that absorbed an entire industry. They recognize it is one thing for the Government to control the railroads as a wartime measure or to encourage the cooperation of an entire industry, such as steel, copper or oil, as a wartime unit and quite another story for all the railroads or steel mills or copper mines or oil wells to be directed by a single private head for private profit in times of peace.

Big business has learned that some competition is desirable. It is more than reconciled to the abandonment of the old trust idea, such as the complete control of the oil industry by John D. Rockefeller and the railroads by E. H. Harriman. It is actually afraid of any attempt to restore these former imperial ambitions. But it does want large units, very large units, in industry.

For one thing the immensely increased cost of labor and materials requires larger capital. A small insurance company might have provided insurance for a large consignment of cotton at ten cents a pound, but it becomes difficult for a concern with small resources to insure much cotton at thirty cents a pound. Then, too, if the expected competition with Europe after the war materializes, no industry will be able to stand for the pace unless it is made up of large, strong working units. But big business has learned from the sad school of experience that there is a point beyond which combination ceases to be efficient.

"I see no reason why the Midvale and Baldwin companies should merge," says one of the country's leading capitalists a few weeks ago in discussing the rumor then prevalent that a deal between these two great concerns was imminent. "There is

nothing physically or legally impractical about such a merger,"
he continued: "but why should they merge? Each is so large
now and has so much business that it cannot handle what it has.
No man is able to handle a unit larger than each of these has
now become."

21   *Ben Hecht*
                         How's Chicago Now?

A skillful writer characterizes the mood of Chicago in wartime.

Chicago has a definite war characteristic. A throng of Chicagoans lining the curbs and watching a file of recruits marching away to the training camps and the front is distinguishable
from a similar throng in New York, Oshkosh or New Orleans.
A crowd of Chicagoans supping in a cafe, riding to work in a
street car, assembled about a fallen horse or stoningly gazing at
the flap-jack turner in a lunch room window has about it an
obvious, an almost racial stamp. This thing which marks Chicago
is, in the light of its military and material contributions to the
struggle, a paradox which causes the city's editorial writers to
emit daily a whimsical despair.

Chicago is calm. It is seemingly indifferent. It does not cheer.
It keeps forgetting to take its hat off when the flag goes by. Its
features are composed, its voice contained. With thousands of
its sons on the battle front, and thousands more on their way,
with thousands of its women plunged over their heads into war
work and with millions of its dollars invested, Chicago, by some
almost inexplicable process of crowd psychology, stands in the
year 1918 an awkward spectator before the pageant of world
strife. A great Allied victory brings no particular visible light
to its face. A vicious German smash does not perceptibly darken

SOURCE. Ben Hecht, "How's Chicago Now?" *Forum* (1918), **60**:181-188.

its eye. Not 3000 but 30,000 miles away does the war seem from its streets. And the distance from the moon to the earth is no greater than the seeming distance from Ypres to the consciousness of the red-faced man with the napkin tucked under his chin studying the bill of fare as the orchestra plays everything but "Die Wacht Am Rhein."

CHICAGO "INDIAN" FACE

This curious mask of silence and indifference distinguishes Chicago today. It is the expression of a people inspired by loyalty rather than idealism. It is the Indian face of the silent Middle West. It is the way of Chicago—a city of detached individualisms, unfused elements, a metropolis of which a full 70 per cent of its residents are men and women born and reared elsewhere. This lack of civic consciousness is at once the curse and the virtue of the town. For while it makes for an indifference toward common causes it breeds self reliance. The war has abruptly brought this latter element to the surface. Chicago in the grip of modern upheaval is a city of efficient smooth functioning units, with a work in common but each holding his emotion separate, his spirit unfused, his grief and joy individual. . . .

In this particular war worker's complaint is contained one of the explanations of the city's apparent emotional lethargy. Whatever the war may be to the Europeans and to other sections of America, the war to Chicago is business. It is superbusiness, spectacular, a traffic in ideals. But it is the training and habit of Chicagoans to work, to think and to feel alone. And so to each man and woman working, giving, sacrificing in a common cause the war still remains an individual matter. His Red Cross contribution is an individual contribution, his Liberty Bond purchase an individual investment, his son's or his brother's absence from the home a personal anxiety, pride or grief. He has not learned to think in crowds, to pool his enthusiasm with his neighbor's. He is dedicated wholeheartedly and unstintingly to the war, but his dedication is a private thing, his patriotism a private thrill. "John Brown's Body Lies a Mouldering in the Grave" and not "The Marsellaise" is the song of the Middle

West—an Indian chant, quiet and vast, like the waving of fields of corn. . . .

PLEDGE OF THE "INDIAN" FACE

Are they ashamed to show their enthusiasm, to reveal their tears, to flash their spirit before each other? The casualty lists have started coming back. Already pictures of heroes who a month or so ago were tending the butcher shops, the dry goods counters and the factory benches of the town begin to appear in the daily papers. The great men of the city—its bankers, politicians, financiers, Upham, Reynolds, Field, Sullivan, Billings, Rosenwald—have emerged from their inconspicuous offices to do their share. Look closely and you will see Red Cross shops filled with women who wear service star pins on their bosoms. You will see canteens in the Public Library, in the department stores, office buildings, along the Lake Shore. In the Defense Council building in Adams street you will find a thousand executives, male and female, for all walks of life, organizing the vast mufti army of the state. Inspect the National record. There you will behold the spirit of Chicago translated into terms of men and money.

And yet . . . down the street comes the Twenty Eighth District —a running line of youths bobbing along with women at their sides and children in their arms and the inevitable assortment of suitcases in their hands. The banners over their heads proclaim they are heading for Berlin. A band precedes them filling the air with a roar of music . . . . Down the street comes the Twenty Eighth District of the Honor Army—men who a day ago were working as you and I, minding their own business. And here they are, familiar faces and still in familiar civilian clothes, marching away to the great adventure in France and Italy and Flanders. It is the rush-hour—six o'clock—and the sidewalks are jammed. The throngs pushing home, read, stop and watch. The lone handkerchief of a belated stenographer flutters from a high window. Some one cries out "Yip, 'Atta boy!" The marchers begin to sing, a sturdy, discordant medley that rises above the blare of the band. The traffic cop clears the way for them. The

Twenty Eighth District draft turns the corner. No sound of cheer of wild farewell, no demonstrations. Chicago watches them away, interested, unmoved. But the quiet bland face of the throng is the "Indian" face of the silent Middle West turned with the pledge of life and all toward the battle.

22 *Dudley Glass*
How's Atlanta Now?

The writer's depiction of the mood in Atlanta differs vastly from that of Chicago, a reminder of the pluralistic nature of American society, although both cities were dedicated to the war effort.

Atlanta is taking the war seriously but not tearfully; she is sorry it had to be, but joyous at having a part in it. She sent her boys away with silken flags flying, and she is devoting herself now to taking the boys from other towns into her heart and showing them that she loves a soldier. There is no mourning in Atlanta, though the gold stars have replaced the blue on many a service flag in the windows of her homes; there is only rejoicing that the Americans are pressing on toward the Rhine and the hope that the Allies will make no peace until they have carried the flag to Berlin.

It is Atlanta's way to meet great situations joyously, exuberantly, and to "carry on" with a song. Atlanta will never admit that she can be injured by fire or flood or prestilence. She has accepted the hardships of war with a grin of good-humor; she has taken the profits where she could, though they have been few, for there have been no great war contracts here. She has given to the Red Cross and the Red Triangle; she has subscribed to the Liberty Loans; but she declines to be down-hearted. . . .

SOURCE. Dudley Glass, "How's Atlanta Now?" *Forum* (1918), **60**:603–612.

THE SOUTH MORE AMERICAN THAN "SOUTHERN"

We have never been sorry we were at war, I think. The South has been inclined to look upon Woodrow Wilson as little short of infallible. When he advocated watchful waiting, we waited and watched, albeit with some impatience. When he decided that the time for waiting was over, we rejoiced openly. Our eighteen months of war have brought us regulation and restriction which stepped hard upon the toes of our traditional states' right conviction, but the one or two politicians who tried to make capital of opposition to the administration learned that the South was more American than Southern. Witness the defeat of Senator Hardwick of Georgia, one of the most popular of her sons. President Wilson had only to intimate that he preferred the election of a more friendly candidate. The next week Senator Hardwick was buried in the discard.

We are not glad we are at war. But we are not moping over it. We are sending our young men overseas to fight beside the young men of New England and the West for the honor and glory of the United States, and we are sending them with a song on our lips, though our eyes may be dim with tears. We present them with silken colors, embroidered by the hands of young girls, and our regiments—where there are regiments that maintain an identity—have girl "sponsors" to bid them good bye. For we are very proud in the South of the boys who go to fight, and we are not ashamed to display our pride. There is none of Chicago's "Indian face" in Atlanta. We cheer wildly when the colors go waving by, and our hats are off when the bands play "The Star Spangled Banner." We are even learning to stand up when the musicians play "The Marsellaise," if some one who recognizes the air gives us the example. . . .

LABOR INDIFFERENT AND INDEPENDENT IN
EXCESSIVE PROSPERITY

But the labor situation has reached a point so serious that it forms the topic of discussion wherever two or three men or women meet. We have depended upon the Negro for our physical labor and our house work. There was a time when a dollar a day obtained the services of a pick wielder or an odd-job man, but that is in the dim past. The wage rose to a dollar and a half a long time ago. But nowadays the Negro man will not consider working for less than three dollars a day, while the untrained servant girl demands five dollars a week and her meals for washing dishes and sweeping the floors. We wouldn't protest so much, perhaps, if we could keep them, even at those wages. But here is where the peculiar disposition of the Negro comes in.

The Negro—and I am writing of the Negro as a class and not of the many individual Negroes who are thrifty and ambitious—desires a place to sleep, no matter how dirty and insanitary and generally uncomfortable, an outfit of gaudy clothing, and three meals, and he is not, as ordinarily supposed, a gargantuan eater. Six dollars a week will buy him those essentials to happiness. Therefore, he works two days a week and spends the remaining five sauntering up and down Decatur street declaring his independence of the white man. The servant girl comes when she pleases and goes when the spirit moves her and half the households in Atlanta are servantless at least three days of every week. Electric washing machines and kitchen labor-saving devices have had a big sale in Atlanta this year, and the number of businessmen who breakfast at Childs, is remarkable in a city where half-a-dozen restaurants had a hard time to keep going a few years ago, owing to the Southerner's preference for home cooking and his habit of going home to luncheon even if it required two hours.

We must continue to depend upon the Negro, however, for there is no substitute in the South, where the population is almost entirely of Anglo-Saxon or Scotch-Irish descent and there is no such thing as a white servant class. Atlanta is especially American. There is no other city of its size which has such a small proportion of citizens of foreign birth or immediate descent. We have a colony of Greeks, but they own and operate the restaurants and fruitstands and call no man master. We have a little Russia, but its inhabitants conduct cheap stores in the Negro districts and build up tidy fortunes thereby. We had hardly enough Germans to support a Turn Verein in the period before the war and the day after we entered the was there was none. We have no Scandinavians, no Irish of the emigrant type, and the Jamaican Negro has not yet learned there are elevators to be operated in our apartment houses and hotels. We must hire a Southern darky or do the work ourselves. We are learning to do it, too. One of our wealthiest bankers telephoned a few days ago to say he would be absent from a directors' meeting because he was plowing his farm. The manager of one of our big stores invites his friends out to his suburban home to see the new electric laundry he has installed in his basement, where he does the week's washing every Monday afternoon after business hours. And it is an ordinary thing to see a limousine built for a chauffeur being driven by the head of the family while his wife and her guests at a theater party sit behind the glass screen and communicate with him by means of the speaking tube.

ATLANTA WANTS THE WAR WON IN GERMANY

We have had our share of everything the war has brought except spy scares and explosions. We gave up our annual season of Metropolitan Opera, upon which we had prided ourselves for eight years. We have contented ourselves with one teaspoonful of sugar in our breakfast coffee, though Southerners have a sweet tooth; we have sat on our verandas through a succession of sunny and inviting gasolineless Sundays; we have even faced iceless days in midsummer. An unprecedented drouth which has emptied the reservoirs in the mountains has curtailed our electric service and made our Great White Way as dark as a cavern and stopped half our elevators. And as I write this we are in the midst of an influenza scare which has closed the theaters and motion picture houses and prohibited all public gatherings, though the Southeastern Fair is in full swing and drawing larger throngs than ever before. We are feeling something more serious than that, now our boys are in the thick of the fighting over there. The great division we sent overseas from Camp Gordon included thousands of Atlanta boys; young officers just graduated from the training school, boys drafted from every home, and the news has come that this division was in the great drive at St. Mihiel. There are many gold stars on the service flags which dot our streets. There were scores of gold stars carried by women in black in the service parade which marked the opening of our Liberty bond campaign. There is never a casualty list which does not bring a pang to some Atlanta home.

But Atlanta is taking the war joyously, for all that, and bravely. And over all the city is the conviction that this war should be won on German soil. The German acceptance of President Wilson's terms came over the wires a few days ago, and Atlanta, instead of rejoicing that the war appeared nearing its end, was indignant at the thought that our American soldiers who had sailed overseas to give the Hun the beating he deserved should be cheated of the opportunity to administer it.

FARM, WORKSHOP, AND GHETTO

23   *Charles Moreau Harger*
            The Farmer and Three-Dollar Wheat

The wheat farmers of the Middle West became highly irritated at government price fixing which restricted profits during a period of high demand. As had happened often in the past, farmers benefited less than other occupational groups under conditions of general prosperity.

Six farmers stood near their wheat wagons at a Middle West cooperative elevator waiting to "weigh in" their loads of grain. The scales were out of order and they gathered in a little group discussing the wheat situation, the subject uppermost in their minds. Each wagon held 50 bushels or more—a clean $100 a load at the price paid at that station.

"It's not enough, compared with other things," declared Jim Haywood. Like his neighbors, he was fairly successful, take it one year with another, and a hard worker. "The government took money out of my pocket and hurt nobody else when it fixed the price of wheat, and I can't see that it was right."

"But $2 a bushel is a good figure," interrupted Sandy McRae, noted for his thriftiness. "I hauled wheat here in the summer of 1914 for 64 cents a bushel. Two dollars is good money."

"Maybe it is," continued Jim, "but that don't answer it. You've

SOURCE. Charles M. Harger, "The Farmer and Three-Dollar Wheat," *Scribner's Magazine* (1918), 64:80–86.

got money in the bank. Suppose you were like me. Suppose you were in debt $3,000 on a 160-acre farm, had only a fair amount of livestock, barely enough implements, and for two years had only broke even because of crop failure. You raised 100 acres of wheat last season, averaging 18 bushels to the acre and of good grade. Figuring up, it had cost you $300 for the seed, $4 a day for harvest hands, 10 cents a bushel for threshing, and was worth at the elevator $2.75 a bushel—it might even go to $3 a little later. Deducting your expense, you could figure for your labor and use of the land a return of $4,000—and it would look mighty good to you. Then one morning came news that the government had fixed the price of wheat at $2 a bushel at your market, wiping out $1,350 of your income. How would you feel about it?"

That was what happened to the wheat farmer in the autumn of 1917, and for nine months he has endeavored to reconcile his financial disappointment with his patriotism. All this time he has been the subject of a flood of news and editorial comment ranging from laudation to abuse. Because he accepted the nation's dictum without starting organized opposition, he has been heralded as a philanthropist; because he questioned the justice of the regulation he has been railed at as a profiteer.

. Were it merely a matter of that one crop, the agitation would already have passed into history, for a new harvest is here. But from that same farmer must come a large part of the foodstuffs for the Allies and upon him depends the number of wheatless days we shall have in the winter of 1919-20. Never before has the American farmer been held responsible for the season's return. He has sown little or much as conditions favored; whether the world over averaged the yield; transportation equalized the supply, and the nations were fed. Now it is vitally important whether or not he decides to sow an increased acreage.

"Well, what are you going to do about sowing next fall?" put in Miles Minter, whose farm joined Sandy's on the east. "Going to put in more or less?"

"Haven't decided yet," was the reply, "but I suppose I'll do about the same as usual. I'm not kicking on the government and am willing to help the war—but I don't think the wheat farmer should be the only one regulated. There's plenty of others need it."

"Last fall I wanted to be patriotic," added Squire Taylor, who had been quietly listening, "and besides the price looked good—it was $2.80 at one time—and we were guaranteed $2; so I put in an extra 80 acres. Half of it winter killed. Don't think I will sow quite so much this year—my boy has gone to the army and it's some job to get a hired man these times. Besides, there's other crops that pay better. Wheat at $2 a bushel here isn't any bonanza, but I'll do all I can, I'll tell you that."

"So will I," agreed Haywood, "but you can't make me believe that it's fair to pick out the wheat farmer and regulate his crop —without helping him to get his implements on a basis of his wheat price—and not touch the cotton grower. Treat us all alike. Why should the wheat raiser be the goat?" The others nodded approvingly. Jim had summarized the attitude of the average producer of the Middle West. . . .

The truth is that the wheat farmer is neither a profiteer nor entirely self-sacrificing. He is in business to earn for himself and his family a living and to lay aside something for old age. He is not a plutocrat—the farm-mortgage debt of the United States is nearly $4,000,000,000. His prosperity has flourished in proportion to his expenditure of labor and brains. Success and failure mingle in every community. His income during the war period has been unquestionably the greatest in his history because the price level of his products has been high. But so has the income of other businessmen. His returns have been exaggerated because the products of the farm are visible. His neighbors know almost to the dollar what he receives for his year's toil. He must meet the rising expenses of his farm. If he raise corn and rye and oats instead of wheat it will be because he feels that he can secure a larger income thus, and his duty to his family demands that he undertake those things most promising and not because he is unpatriotic.

Abuse will not change the farmer's mind. Criticism will not induce greater effort. Fully independent and confident of his position, the man on the plough is thinking things out for himself. Daily papers are left at the mail-box of nearly every rural home, and their readers are as well informed of the progress of world affairs as the dweller on city streets. They draw their conclusions as to the opportunities and accomplishments of other lines of business.

Here and there are communities where indifference to the nation's needs seems to exist, but on analysis it will generally be found it is merely an expression of firm conviction that wheat alone should not have had a price established by governmental action. The solution will come through such readjustment as will appeal to the business judgment of these producers, who after all understand fully the exigency of the world's demands and can do much to relieve it. Generally, however, over the agricultural States is a sound Americanism eager to uphold the hands of the country. It is not effusive. No parades pass the farm, no banners or bunting decorate the country highways, no bands are playing. Amid the quiet of the broad fields the worker must visualize the panoply of war. . . .

The six farmers waiting by the elevator were types of the wheat-producing class, each with a somewhat different point of view and each with his own home problems to solve. But not a man in the group was disposed to act in a resentful spirit or with any other inclination than to help his government—though feeling that he must consider at the same time the welfare of his family and himself and that limitations of labor supply and physical endurance surround him.

Back of all the discussion and of the imperative considerations of our strength and safety this fundamental truth stands: the farmer has the nation's weal at heart and to the extent of his ability will be a good soldier, the soldier of the wheatfield—as important today as the soldier of the field of battle.

24   *Aaron Hardy Ulm*
A Two Billion Dollar Cotton Crop

*The writer draws attention to the importance of cotton in the south-
ern economy but shows that the war had lessened regional dependence
on its principal export commodity. He draws the moral of this change
for the South generally.*

No commercial romance or tragedy of all the war is more
unique than that of cotton. Less than three years ago it was
without a market; hardly more than two years ago it had to
plead for 7 cents a pound; ten months ago it brought nearly 22
cents a pound; then it dropped to 13; then it came back in midsummer, 1917, when it reached 27 cents; and in a year it may. . . .

When the diplomatists gather to retouch the world's physiog-
nomy and define the beginning of a new age, a product of
mother earth in the uppermost thoughts of those shrewd gamblers
for advantage will be cotton. Commerce more than geography
will prompt thought and action at that greatest of diplomatic
congresses. There will be no dream of commercial conquest in
which cotton won't be a dominant figure; and the most baffling
nightmare to all Europe's players for commercial vantage will
be Dixie Land.

For our own South is supplying the bulk of the world's raw
cotton and whatever the future may portend or make possible
from Dixie must be drawn most of the staple with which the
world's textile trade will be reorganized. That trade is a most
significant factor in world commerce. With it has gone commercial empire. It might be said without great exaggeration that
the flag follows the shirt. Around it dominance in the Pacific
revolves, together with trade supremacy in South America—

SOURCE. Aaron Hardy Ulm, "A Two Billion Dollar Cotton Crop," *Forum*
(1917), **58**:333-344.

which questions will haunt, as few others will, the room where the biggest iron dice ever rattled by diplomats will decide the course of centuries. . . .

What of the future?

Dixie has the whip hand. Southern spots have sold steadily above New York futures. Many times during the past year the slack in futures was taken up by Southern spots refusing to sag. As indicated by Secretary McAdoo, in justifying government aid to Southern growers in 1914, cotton is as staple as gold. It is imperishable. Strands of lint taken recently from old Egyptian tombs were as pliable as new fibre. William B. Dana long ago said that cotton combined all the qualities of a legal tender to a greater degree than any other commodity except gold.

Financial recoupment, brought about through industrial progress and given virility by the Federal Reserve banking act, enables the Dixie farmer to finance his cotton crop. He can "hold" indefinitely. In recent years vast warehouses wherein the staple may be stored cheaply have been constructed throughout the belt. A receipt from a bonded warehouse is as good at a Southern bank as a government bond. . . .

You may ask: what of the future South, that land so romantically, so traditionally identified with cotton? What of the South 40, 50, 75 years hence, when railroads and irrigation will be turning the plateaus of Trans-Caucasia, the pampas of the Paraguay and Parana, the plains of Uganda and the wide sweeps of mysterious China into fields of blossoming white?

It is a picture more bizarre than threatening. As many have long believed, the South not only would have been better off in the past but would be in the future—without cotton. But for cotton Dixie's splendid history would not be darkened by the last shadow of chattel slavery. There would have been no Civil War. That passing provincialism which held the South's thought aloof from the world at large and caused its people to be unjustly misunderstood is due to cotton.

And that poverty and ignorance, which as a Southerner I refer to in sadness and solely out of fidelity to truth, which renders the people in some remote communities of the South objects of pity such as we feel for few spots in the New or Old World, can be traced to cotton's strange fondness for extremes. And about all of big quality that can be credited to it is a distinctive civilization (modernized by the blood of brothers), the relics and memories of which will ever charm historians and romanticists; and a foreign trade for a new nation.

Those blue months of early fall, 1914, demonstrated more than was apparent. The Prussian bayonet had caused the South's business structure to reel. The South stood in awe, dazed. Though famine dared put forth its fearful threat, the South didn't tremble or lose its nerve. For the South could have thrown every bale of cotton into the sea, burned every ginhouse, destroyed every cotton seed and interjected further planting of cotton, and still would have been in better financial and commercial situation, aye, by fifty times, than at the close of the Civil War. For the South has outgrown cotton. Relatively, cotton is in the minority. Though it still dominates Southern finance, being a product peculiarly financial, it no longer tyrannizes Southern commerce, except in a remotely banking sense. It is. exceeded in volume by the production of foodstuffs. The value of the South's manufactures double it. Combine lumber, minerals, naval stores, tobacco, fruits, and a score of products in which the section is leading or might lead, and you have a commercial giant by which cotton would be a pigmy. Then remember that all these are "infant industries"; that the industrial South is in its childhood; that its natural wealth has hardly been "discovered," much less massed for development—and you find that cotton can be eliminated and leave a land rich in fact and in prospect.

A suspicion of all this is creeping into the mind of the Southerner and is influencing his attitude toward the nation and the world. For a hundred and twenty years the mainspring of political and business opinion in the South was cotton. Unravel the often complicated texture of Southern sentiment and you find the binding thread was ever cotton.

It is so no longer. Great Britain's declaration of war on Germany was apparently the heaviest blow ever dealt cotton. Yet the South was with Great Britain. The British embargo delayed as to cotton out of deference to Southern opinion but put into full effect in 1915 cost the South ·hundreds of millions of dollars. There was some ground for the argument that the embargo was illegal. Still the South made no protest—it really approved the move and was glad to contribute its losses to the cause it now joins in openly espousing. Efforts to arouse sentiment there against the embargo, made by able men whose leadership is usually accepted, brought forth general condemnation. The South's opinion rose above the interests of cotton. For the South at last is independent—even of cotton, its king and former tyrant, though King Cotton now occupies his throne more majestically than ever before.

25   Samuel Gompers
Right Makes Might

The President of the American Federation of Labor argues that the onset of the war should not prejudice the eight-hour day and good working conditions. Like many other advocates of interest groups, the labor leader identified the objectives of his clientele with the cause of democracy.

As our national crisis became steadily more and more acute, it became more and more clear that no practical program of defense could be adopted and executed without the cooperation of the men and women who use the tools. For tools are the basic agencies of our civilization.

In no previous war has organized labor had a direct part to play. In no previous war has organized labor had representatives in the councils authorized to deal with the conduct of war. For this war is one in which the armies and navies at the front are dependent, as is civilization itself, on the men and women in the factories and fields. It is clearly just as essential to protect all these auxiliaries at home from baneful economic and industrial evils as it is to safeguard the lives of the men at the front. Nothing

SOURCE: Samuel Gompers, "Right Makes Might," *Independent* (1917) 92:282.

could be more evident. Labor must see to it, as part of patriotic duty, that the rights of working people be kept at heart. The experience of England shows how necessary it is that this thought be kept clearly in mind. We must profit by that experience.

And further than that:

We have heard the claim that democracy is not and cannot be efficient.

With the people of the United States rests the responsibility of demonstrating that democracy, as exemplified in America, can— in war as well as in peace—prove itself to be efficient.

To make this country efficient in the highest degree cooperation between the agencies of the Government and particular units is necessary. That cooperation is dependent very largely upon the men and women who handle the tools. I think the great lesson to be got from English experience is that cooperation in the form of good results cannot be got from underfed workingmen and women. They must be paid enough to permit them to live decently. They must not be asked to work over eight hours a day, six days a week. They must not be asked to work unnecessarily in unhealthful conditions.

Of course, if you want to get all there is in men in the shortest possible time, work them twenty-four hours a day. You can do that two days in succession. But at the end of the second day they will be worthless.

This democracy will prove itself most efficient if it does not ask its workingmen and workingwomen to work more than eight hours a day. This fact has, to my mind, been amply demonstrated. Many of our ablest employers have laid it down as a law that labor shall not be asked to work more than six days a week, eight hours a day.

The eight-hour-day six-days-a-week rule—so Mr. Ford and many other manufacturers have demonstrated—is a principle. It is no longer debatable. To break away from such a principle in a time of stress such as this would be to display enterprize instead of judgment and to prove that in time of war democracy as exemplified in America stands ready to defeat its own ends.

It has also been established as a principle that good working conditions—good light, sanitation, etc.—are essential to maximum output.

In a word, good working conditions are as essential to high production as high production in this time of stress is essential to the maintenance of a battlefront. It would seem to be treason to the best interests of this country to desert such principles now. Now more than at any time in our national history we do not want production to fall off; rather, we want to accentuate it. Now more than ever we want the army in the factories and fields to be an army of strength, fighting for democracy; we don't want a nation of working people with hearts and bodies weakened. We need, rather to strengthen our men and women for the war and for the reconstruction after the war.

It is on these grounds that the committee of which I am the head recommended to the Council of National Defense the adoption of resolutions urging the maintenance of existing legislative and administrative standards. The adoption of this resolution, coming just at a time when not a few efforts were being made to induce legislatures to repeal laws that had been got with difficulty and when other attempts were being made to take advantage of our national situation, was most salutary.

For war is the open season of a large class of unpatriotic persons who are ready to make the best of all opportunities afforded by national distress. Our committee has an enormous program directed to the carrying out of this resolution and to the mobilization of every possible ounce of labor energy, to the end that the world "may be made safe for democracy."

The supreme thought that I have in cooperating and in asking the cooperation of the men of labor in America is to demonstrate that democracy does not spell inefficiency, but, on the contrary, to demonstrate that the democracy of America can show to the whole world that in war as in peace it is united for any emergency.

26   *Florence C. Thorne*
                            Women and War Service

The author discusses the consequences of the war for female workers and advocates "equal pay for equal work" as a logical consequence of the nation's war aims.

Out of restriction and repression into opportunity is the meaning of the war to thousands of women. A development that was taking place slowly now becomes conspicious when accelerated by the driving necessities of war. In those countries where social organization has been adjusted to meet war needs and purposes there is no room for the parasitic and all the "conspicuous consumption" class.

Common danger is a great leveling force that has swept aside the sham and the useless—there is no time or place for the idler or the doer of useless work. Every individual must do his bit of real work and assume his share of responsibility—women and men share alike the common danger and need. Each must work where his or her individual service will count most. In returning to more primitive conditions where men must fight and women must work, much of the artificiality of life disappears.

The fact that women are going out to do the world's work together with men is not in itself an undesirable development. Work is a means of self-expression and development for women as well as men. Work for pay means economic independence which is the only basis for real freedom of any kind. Freedom in the economic world gives women opportunity to choose their own lives and protects them from being forced into marriage for economic reasons.

SOURCE. Florence C. Thorne, "Women and War Service," *New Republic* (June 1917), 455–456.

The real problem that confronts us at our entrance into the war is not to resist the entrance of women into industry but so to direct and control the movement that women will be benefited and that their men fellow-workers will not be injured. The necessity for prompt, firm action to this end is already manifest.

When the freight handlers of the Washington Terminal went on strike, the management filled their places from among the men on the force and then filled the office positions formerly held by men with women who went to work for lower salaries. These women, many of them unconsciously, were virtually used as strike breakers.

The Pennsylvania Railroad has been making extensive experiment to determine in what positions women may be substituted for men in order that men may be released for military service. Other managers of offices, such as prominent bankers, have announced beforehand that they intended to expedite enlistment by making arrangements to employ women clerks in the place of men. Many have announced, however, that they did not purpose to pay women the same salaries as was paid the men. From this it is evident that one of the immediate and vital problems that must be met is this purpose to exploit women by paying them lower wages than are paid to men doing the same work.

The methods and purposes of business for private profit did not change overnight with the declaration of war between the United States and Germany. Both men and women must be protected against exploitation of this kind. The one provision that can assure this protection is equal pay for equal work. When women refuse to work more cheaply than men, financial interests will not direct employers to substitute women for men but to choose from among both men and women upon a basis of value of service.

It is clear that in the months to come women will enter industry and business life in rapidly increasing numbers. Conscription for war service creates a new work that only men can perform while at the same time makes more imperative continuous output from industry and commerce and operation of transportation agencies. Women must do their part of this work essential to the nation's success in winning the war, but their work must be directed and organized in accord with standards of physical welfare, self-respect, and freedom. Women will have to work out their own salvation—they cannot depend upon men for this. This necessitates intelligent self-interest and cooperation among women. If women direct their entrance into the business world intelligently and organize industrial relationships equitably, they can avert long and needless struggles against established injustice. This is work to be done by women's organizations, together with the trade unions of men.

One effort of the women to deal with this problem is very promising. When the United Cigar Stores Company of New York City began to make provisions for women to take the places of men who might desire to enlist for the war, they asked representatives of the Women's Suffrage Party if they could furnish women. These representatives replied they could if the women who took the men's places should receive the same pay as a man would receive taking the same place. This means that a woman beginner would be paid the same as a man beginner. The Women's Suffrage Party, through its War Service Enrollment Bureau, will help to fill vacancies from the lists of women enrolled with them. The women will first be trained in the school of salesmanship conducted by the United Cigar Stores Company and be given pay while being instructed in their duties. Their pay will be increased as they become more proficient exactly with the pay of men similarly employed.

In this national emergency upon women will fall men's responsibilities as well as men's work. They can fulfill their obligations only when given equal pay.

It would be unwise to look upon this development of the war as temporary—to be met with makeshifts. Many of the men will go to the firing line never to return. Women's responsibilities will be permanent.

The jagged furrows the war will cut across the nations involved in it will mean a new world at the close of the war. It is idle to imagine that prewar conditions can ever be re-established—probably it would be unwise to desire. Changes are whirling fast upon changes. If the war is worth the fighting, these changes ought to count for liberty and democracy. Changes ought to be in furtherance of permanent ideals.

Instead of clinging to the past, we ought to plan boldly for a splendid world after the war—a world of new-found liberty where each shall assume full responsibility for their own lives.

True women have no desire to shirk responsibility or duty as mothers of the race, but they demand the right to give their performance of duty moral value possible only when the volition is assured.

The slogan "Equal pay for equal work" which women have raised to protect their interests at this time is in furtherance of the highest ideals of womanhood. It expresses self-respect, conscious of ability to render service, jealously guarding dignity against undervaluation in the eyes of others.

Women want to give service to the nation but they want that service to be something more than exploitation. If sacrifice is made, it ought to profit the nation not private gain.

27   *Ordway Tead*
The New Place of Labor

The author discusses the newfound power and prestige of the organized labor movement, a consequence of the war, and the implications of this development for the future. His optimism proved legitimate in the long run, but the twenties just ahead were lean years for many workers.

Labor has won a new place in American life in the last twelve months. The workers have been accorded unprecedented recognition in the conduct of public affairs. The leaders of organized labor have been called to Washington, not merely to advise, but actively to administer, and the rank and file of workers, especially in the war industries, have secured concessions in the principles and terms of labor-adjustment for which they

SOURCE. Ordway Tead, "The New Place of Labor," *Atlantic Monthly* (1918), 122:178–185. Reprinted from *The Atlantic Monthly,* Boston, Mass.

had struggled unsuccessfully for a decade.

No one who visualizes the protean diversity of American conditions believes that American labor is about to take the reins of government into its hands or that there is a unified host of a myriad manual workers advancing with clear aims under a common banner. The situation in a working class of thirty million people is not so simple. But when, as is the case today, a point of vantage has been reached, it is important to define the changes and to get a sense of the direction which liberated forces and new tendencies are taking.

Unquestionably the Wilson administration has been sympathetic with organized labor. There is no other way to account for the amity which has been characteristic of the government's relations with the workers at the navy yards and arsenals. Organized as these workers are into a number of craft unions, it has been possible for Secretaries Daniels and Baker to adjust all matters in a way which has precluded practically all strikes at government plants. . . .

Significant in the development of the new national attitude toward labor has been the report of the President's Mediation Commission. Its trip into the West in the late fall brought it face to face with less than a dozen impending controversies. Yet so critical were the issues involved in each of these that the recommendations of the commission carry special weight. Its report adds its support to the great tide of opinion favoring the eight-hour day; it declares unequivocally for the necessity of collective bargaining as the only means by which the power of workers and employers can be approximately equalized and the suppressed and thwarted impulses in working-class life be given free and positive play. The commission left behind it, in each of the districts which it investigated, agencies for the joint control and determination of controverted issues. . . .

There have, in short, emerged, in the numerous efforts to cope with the labor problem for war purposes, a variety of suggestions for a national labor policy. The demand for a formulated declaration upon many of these matters became more and more widespread, and in response to it President Wilson appointed the so-called Taft-Walsh Board, of five employers, five labor leaders, and Messrs. William Howard Taft and Frank P.

Walsh, to frame a labor policy for the nation. Its unanimous recommendations have all been in the direction we are tracing. They declare for the right of labor to organize and to bargain collectively; for the basic eight-hour day; for the collating, through the unions and the United States employment service, of information about skilled workers available for the war industries; for the fixing of minimum wages which shall "insure the subsistence of the worker and his family in health and reasonable comfort"; and for the appointment of a National War Labor Board, selected in the same manner as the policy-determining board. The function of this new body is to adjust all disputes for the settlement of which no other machinery exists or is created. . . .

What more can be asked?

Nothing more will be asked by those who are looking so intently at today that they forget tomorrow. For the emergency the nation is—with certain important exceptions—prepared. But for the emergence, for the turgid period of reconstruction, for the generation of democratic expansion that will follow the war —are we prepared for that? The question is raised, not to distract attention from immediate military issues, not to belittle the value of what has been done. It is raised because the facts of labor's present position, influence, and purposes point inevitably to a new dispensation. A new generation in the labor world, studying zealously the reconstruction lessons which British labor is teaching, is forcing us to find an answer. We shall win the war, is the claim of the younger labor leaders, not alone by invincible efforts on the "frontier of freedom" but by simultaneous assault—or at least reconnoitring parties—against antidemocratic forces at home.

Whether this be true or not, the fact is that the position and temper of the workers in America today is very different from what it was a year ago. Problems that had no place, except in the trade-union local or the college economics class, are fast becoming matters for national statesmanship. Labor after the war is certain to exert an influence in determining the direction of reconstruction which is not yet widely appreciated. The problem of industrial government will be forced upon public attention until a solution is at least attempted, if not assured. The only question is, to what extent the other progressive elements in the community will join with labor to clarify its purposes and give form and substance to its aspirations. . . .

Reconstruction becomes but the continuation of a national moral enterprise begun a century and a half ago. Yet there is this difference. We seek today the extension of representative government, not only into politics but into industry. The workers are anxious that, consistently throughout the whole fabric of American life, our common efforts shall contribute to the rearing of a great community wherein shall dwell a happy people disciplined for the fullness of freedom.

28   *Kingsley Moses*
          The Negro Comes North

The war stimulated a massive migration of Negroes from the South to more northerly communities in which employment in industry suddenly became available. This development greatly expanded the number and size of Negro ghettoes in the great urban centers of industrial America, particularly in the Boston-Washington-Chicago triangle.

If within the space of six months every man, woman, and child should leave the city of Boston and wander away to the ends of the earth, so startling an exodus would occasion the most excited comment. If Baltimore, or either of the great states of Oregon or Maine were similarly deserted, there would arise a world-wide sensation. Yet since late last summer no less tremendous a migration, numerically at least, has been going on in those states of the old South bounded by the Potomac, Ohio, and Mississippi. For the most conservative figures estimate that during this comparatively short time between six and seven hundred thousand

SOURCE. Kingsley Moses, "The Negro Comes North," *Forum* (1917), 58:181–190.

Negroes have left their native homes and trailed northward in a straggling, haphazard, but never ending stream. . . .

The Negro in the rural districts and small towns of the South, knowing nothing of any other way of life, has no ambitions; indeed, as the days of the Ku Klux, the Red Shirts, and other less well-ordered bands of vigilantes demonstrated during that shameful period of our national history so sardonically termed "Reconstruction," ambition was for the Negro distinctly a dangerous thing. Naturally happy, care-free, and good-humored, the Negro has seemed perfectly satisfied with his lot, and has grinned and laughed all day, and sung and wandered the country-side all night from decade to decade. And, remember, the Southern Negro is never surly and seldom dangerous—never indeed unless driven made by the vile liquor of the "blind tigers." Whether or not he is unjustly treated is a question—although not a question for discussion by those knowing nothing of living conditions in the South—but at any rate he seems, or has seemed until this past year, perfectly content.

And now suddenly, yet withal so quietly that little heed has been given, the Negro begins to move; not individually or apparently thoughtlessly, but deliberately and by the hundreds of thousands.

Late summer and all the winter saw a steady procession of Negroes, big and small, old and young, strong and feeble, man, woman, and child pouring north through the great Union Station at Washington. Here an old "uncle" tottered along under his tightly stuffed pack, fashioned clumsily out of an old bed quilt. Behind him was a vigorous young couple, black as the native Hottentot, trailed by three stumbling youngsters; the woman with a well-wrapped pickaninny at her breast, the man sturdily lugging two heavy straw portmanteaus. Half a dozen mulatto girls, gaudy in the discarded finery of white mistresses, followed, grinning and giggling, pointing at the magnificence of the huge station and venting awed murmurs of: "Lawdy," "Ain't it gran,' " "Mah soul," etc. Then more children, groups of robust men, and whole families laden with trunks, bundles, parcels, and baskets. Morning after morning, evening after evening the motley procession streamed by. And very few returned.

There were, at the time of the last census, approximately ten million Negroes in the United States. Seven million or more of these lived in the South proper—south of the Potomac and east of the Mississippi. Of these six hundred thousand, or at least six per cent, have moved North. Good reasons there must have been for any such general migration.

And, as always, the real reason for the movement was economic. There is precious little fact in the wild tales of general terrorism and habitual bullying and maltreatment that have, from time to time, shrieked themselves forth from certain news columns. The Negroes came, and still come, because they could scarcely make a living in the South while work was abundant in the North.

THE MISCHIEVOUS WEEVIL

Several years ago, over twenty in fact, a noxious little insect commonly known as the Mexican boll weevil, ferried himself across the Rio Grande in some devious manner, and laid his maggotty blight upon the cotton fields of southeastern Texas. The Southerner, ever unconcerned and careless of the future, made at first little effort to check the advance. Texas and Louisiana said: "Oh, well, the Federal Government will soon find a way to stop him." The rest of the cotton states echoed: "Of course it will, see what is happening to the potato bug, the cattle tick, and the plague rots of New Orleans. Anyhow, the weevil can never swim the Mississippi." And yet that is exactly what he did do. Not only did the relentless and devastating little pest jump the big river but he spread himself fast and far over Alabama and Georgia as well, got a firm foothold in Tennessee, and is even now hovering upon the borders of South Carolina with his tiny gray snout pointed directly toward the very northerly rim of the cotton belt of Virginia.

And with the coming of the weevil and the destruction of the cotton crop there suddenly disappeared the means of livelihood of the great mass of the Negroes. Where once fifty hands had been needed for an hundred acre cotton plantation now five or six able-bodied men are amply able to take care of an even larger stock or grain farm. With his big cash cotton crop gone, the planter could no longer provide food for the families of his Negro tenants; and the storekeepers, of course, unanimously refused credit. The tenant farmer could no longer secure provisions on tick from the merchant on expectations of the forthcoming crop; the planter could no longer obtain a credit from his bank on prospective cotton earnings for there was no cotton, there was no crop, and there could be no earnings. . . .

Then, as if by a chance stroke of Providence, came the sudden and frenzied demand for labor in the Northern industrial plants. Necessity knew no law; and, even though it was contrary to the statutes of many Southern states to solicit or export labor, there were plenty of hardy individuals who were willing to risk a heavy fine and probable jail sentence in order to supply their employers with the legions of unskilled labor absolutely necessary for the filling of war orders, the construction of railroads, and the laying down of highways. And these labor agents swarmed over the South as busily and quite as noiselessly as an army of predacious ants.

THE UNDERGROUND RAILWAY

The most enticing offers were extended to the eager and open-mouthed Negroes. Promises of a dollar and a half a day, two dollars—even more—unheard of wealth indeed—were made; long green railway tickets bearing the magical names of New York, Philadelphia, Chicago, and Pittsburg were thrust into willing hands; for the Negro loves the new and strange even more than he loves his home heath—for a time. Less honorable means even were employed, certain roughly printed dodges having brought to the attention of writer the engaging fact that a small town in southern Pennsylvania offers to the Negro the hospitality of five saloons, two free dance halls and street cars without Jim Crow restrictions. The particular dodger did not mention the fact, however, that within the past few years a Negro had been burned at the stake in that very community. . . .

The Underground Railway was again operating; though its passenger agents bore little resemblance to those great-hearted fanatics of the old Slavery days. . . .

Whether the Negro is now better off in the North than in the South cannot be ascertained with any degree of exactness as yet. His advent in such numbers is too recent. But it is a serious problem that may confront the Northern municipalities when the exaggerated demand for labor subsides. What will the Negroes do then? How will the cities take care of the thousands of colored people now engaged in labor than can be at the best but temporary?

THE NEGRO AND ORGANIZED LABOR

The authorities in control of the organized labor elements of the country frown upon the Negro in the skilled industries. It is doubtful that the Negro can affiliate with any, save one of two, of the branches of union labor. In Philadelphia, for example—a town that shows an astounding increase in its colored population—a Negro may be employed to prepare the roadway for the laying of a car line but may not himself place the rails. The North, save in a very few isolated instances, does not countenance the employment of the Negro as a waiter in hotels and clubs—a single house in Boston is, to the writer's knowledge, about the only first class hotel that still maintains Negro service in its dining rooms. Domestic service, it is true, is open to Negro women; but the employment agencies report a comparatively small demand. Public service in police or fire departments is practically closed to the race, only a handful of Negro policemen being employed in New York, Philadelphia, Chicago, and Boston, and these only in solidly Negro districts. The army and navy have room for a few colored men, but prior to the outbreak of hostilities only practically perfect specimens of manhood were considered, and the literary tests bar out the great majority of the applicants. The roughest kind of manual labor in the streets and along the docks is open and presumably will continue to be open to the colored man; and this may be his ultimate resort if foreign immigration is effectively checked off after the war.

In the large, therefore, the opportunity for continual employment at a living wage is the most serious question the Negro must face if he is to remain in the North. And if he cannot get work what is he to do? How will the cities handle him? Not, it is to be hoped, as many of them handled the unemployment problem in the winter of 1913–14 by shunting the able bodied pauper from town to town. . . .

All evidence goes to show that the Negro in proper environment will prove a worthy, peaceable and industrious citizen. The record of the race as a race has been an excellent one, and the North may well profit by the Negro's presence; while the South too benefits, as the difficulty of the race problem is lessened by the withdrawal of the surplus colored population. But it is for the North to open to the Negro enough fields of labor to provide him with the opportunity for a decent livelihood. That done there need be no serious misgivings concerning the colored migration.

29 Report to the Illinois State Council of Defense on the Race Riots at East St. Louis

The Negro migration proved greatly unsettling in many of the urban communities that experienced the sudden influx. The official report of a committee appointed to establish the reasons for one of the most serious racial outbreaks of the period—the affair at East St. Louis in June, 1917—reveals the background.

[T]he riots were due to the excessive and abnormal number of Negroes then, and for some months past, in East St. Louis. The feeling against the colored people originated in two sources, social and labor. There was resentment that the colored people, having overcrowded their quarters, were spreading out into sections of the city regarded as exclusively the precincts of the

SOURCE. "Report to the Illinois State Council of Defense on the Race Riots at East St. Louis by Its Committee on Labor," *American Federationist* (1917), 24:622–625. Reprinted by permission of American Federation of Labor and Congress of Industrial Organization and *American Federationist*.

white people. The colored men, large numbers of whom had been induced there and could find no jobs, in their desperate need were preventing desired improvements being made by labor, and threatening the existing standards of labor, and the white men were resenting it. These facts were set forth in the mayor's first message to the chairman of this Council.

The crisis came at a meeting arranged by the city council to give a public hearing to protest against the situation, which had become intolerable. At that meeting inflammable speeches, which should have been stopped in their midst by the authorities—were made—immediately after that the rioting started.

East St. Louis, with a population of approximately 90,000 has had for a long time a permanent Negro population of from 10,000 to 15,000. This city is, accordingly, accustomed to the presence of colored people in numbers. It is therefore manifest that the trouble was due to the recent rapid influx of the colored people. The evidence shows these came mostly from the southern states. Estimates vary from 6000 to 15,000 as the number that had come within the past year or so. Our investigation accordingly took the line of why they came, since discovery would doubtless suggest the remedy.

For more than two years there has been a considerable migration north of the southern Negro. There has been increased demand for labor in the north on account of the great numbers employed in plants devoted to war materials. This was accentuated by the return of some of the foreigners from the north to their native lands to take their places in the war, and the complete stoppage of the former supply of labor from those countries.

The Negroes from the south furnish the most likely supply to meet this demand because the south pays them lower wages, works them longer hours, gives them less consideration, and surrounds them with poorer working conditions. This movement, so far as it is a result of this condition, is a readjustment of the equilibrium of population in accordance with present economic law, and so far as this is true no issue can be taken with it.

But this committee finds that the situation in East St. Louis differs so much in degree from the situation in most other cities that it could not be explained as a result of ordinary operations. That East St. Louis as accustomed as it is to the presence of colored people could stage a racial outbreak argues that a cause different than ordinary migration of colored labor was operative. Such a cause was definitely established by evidence. It was shown that extensive advertising had been done in southern newspapers, setting forth the allurements in East St. Louis in the way of abundant work, short hours, and high wages, good conditions and treatment. Labor agents were also shown to have been very active in the south. They had gone about soliciting the movement of colored men to East St. Louis. They had invited colored men to assemble in groups of ten in order to get cheaper railroad rates. Excursions by train and by steamboat were offered cheaper for the round trip than the regular one way fare would amount to. That such things were being done was recited in the local press of East St. Louis continually for many weeks and seemed never to be denied.

A peculiarity of this campaign for the importation of unskilled labor to East St. Louis was its anonymous character, a fact in itself suspicious. There appear in all newspapers over the country almost daily advertisements for labor in some other place, which are signed by those who want the employes. Such advertisements, of course, are legitimate. But it seems strange that the extensive territory of the south should be covered by a propaganda urging migration to East St. Louis and at the same time that these advertisements should not only be signed by no one but that they should not designate any particular plant, of which there are many large ones in East St. Louis, that required additional labor. Likewise, labor agents were equally mysterious. It was related that these labor agents would assemble car loads of Negroes and start north accompanying them. At convenient points these agents would leave the car with the remark that they had telegrams to send or would get lunch. They never came back and the train pulled out without them. The Negroes were thus left to shift for themselves upon their arrival in East St. Louis, to find work as they could and quarters as they might.

The evidence warrants the conclusion that there was an extensive campaign to induce Negroes in great numbers to come to East St. Louis. Such a campaign had required considerable financing, and its backers took pains to be unknown. Official recognition of these circumstances was taken in a resolution introduced to the Chamber of Commerce by Mr. M. V. Joyce, its vice-president, ten days before the race riots occurred. The resolution sets fort[h] the things here related and urges that steps be taken to discontinue the practice and to "employ every legitimate means to prevent the influx of Negroes into East St. Louis and thereby take every precaution against crime, riot and disorder generally." The resolution was laid upon the table by the directors of the Chamber of Commerce, pending the forwarding to every member of a copy. The Chamber of Commerce of East St. Louis has within its membership the most influential and the most important, industrially, of its citizenship. The resolution was never acted upon. Its nonaction at a time when the very atmosphere was charged with tense feelings is in line with the anonymous character of the influence bringing the extraordinary influx of Negroes into East St. Louis.

As a result of intense public interest and general discussion of the situation before and after the riots, this committee was confronted with many unverified statements as to conditions existing with relation to the matter to be investigated. It was urged that during the previous year there had been industrial troubles in several of the plants of the city, and that employers had brought about the extraordinary influx of colored men to have a surplus of labor and thus defeat the contentions of their employes. It was alleged that employers had had meetings to arrange a program of importation of the southern Negroes and that the larger employers of the city had collectively been responsible. The managers of all the larger industries of the city were examined and all denied any collusion or knowledge of the campaign conducted in the south to bring Negroes to East St. Louis. The fact remains, however, that these managers were the chief beneficiaries of the surplus of labor and the force of motive points in their direction. Fixing the actual personal responsibility, while it might be desirable, adds nothing at this point. This Council of Defense is a body organized to promote the country's war interests, and to pursue the research for responsibility further along this line would not serve the purpose of this Council. The condition was there, no matter how it was brought about or by whom.

Since this Council is a war body, its endeavors must have a relationship to the war. A harmonious nation is necessary to successful prosecution of war. The situation at East St. Louis, its causes and its consequences, contain a lesson and a warning valuable for guidance in relation to the war. To get the maximum of efficiency for success in this war there must be harmony between capital and labor, between employer and employe. They must face the future with an equal degree of patriotism. Organized labor, in its national central body has, by formal action, inaugurated a policy of suspending or avoiding strikes as far as possible. It thus, as far as possible, waives its right of aggression in making the best bargain possible for its service. This is a most patriotic attitude but in all reason it cannot be expected to maintain that spirit, unless met half way by the employing class. If labor exerts every influence possible to avoid industrial strife, then capital must do the same thing, and must do nothing to impair existing standards of labor.

To import a surplus of labor will promote strife rather than repress it. To so act is not to meet labor half way. Labor has declared a truce, to whatever extent such may be possible, and the employer will be the opposite of a patriot if he does not do the same. Labor has set a patriotic pace which should challenge a patriotic rivalry from the employer. The patriotic spirit of labor thus far has given the government rich promise as to what extent it may be depended upon. This committee therefore recommends the following:

First: That the widest publicity be given to the situation at East St. Louis through the Council of National Defense, and through the respective State Councils of Defense, that the danger in the situations of this kind may be made apparent to the south and the industrial centers of the north, to the end that migration of the southern Negroes may be discouraged before other outbreaks of a similar nature occur.

Second: That migration of any class from one part of the country to another be allowed to flow along natural lines, that the equilibrium of population may not be disturbed; that the severest condemnation should be visited upon those who undertake to promote any artificial movement of population, because such artificial movement is sure to result in friction, and now more than ever should friction be avoided.

Third: That the problems of shifting labor where labor is

needed during the war be handled by the various State Councils
of Defense, in conjunction with the Council of National Defense,
in connection with those responsible officers of the labor movement who are daily showing their patriotism in endeavoring to
restrain industrial strife, and in connection with the Department
of Labor of the United States and similar departments of the
state. It is anticipated that if this is done that labor can be
shifted to where it is needed with sole reference to the benefit of
industry as well as the workers themselves and consequently to
the welfare of the nation.

30   *John Richards*
          Some Experiences with Colored Soldiers

*The use of Negroes in the armed services engendered some sympathy
and respect for the black citizenry, as this article reveals, but even in this
context racial stereotypes appeared on every hand.*

The best of [the Negro soldiers] are very efficient at *liaison*
work, than which there is nothing more important. The mes-
senger must often not only run through hell with his message,
but *get* through. Besides courage and endurance, they had a
marvelous knack of finding their way in the infernal tangle of
an old trench-system which had changed hands several times.
Our best man was one who in civil life had been a distinguished
"gun-man."
   Sickness has a very depressing effect on the Negro: a boy who
suffers with rheumatism is sure that it is going to his heart; a
cold brings thoughts of an early grave, though they are really very
rugged. We had expected much sickness with the cold weather,
yet found, for the most part, nothing worse than imaginings and

SOURCE. John Richards, "Some Experiences with Colored Soldiers," *Atlantic
Monthly* (1919), 124:184–190. Reprinted from *The Atlantic Monthly*, Boston,
Mass.

low spirits. They dropped away fast in the hospital when we were waiting at Brest to go home; but so did their white officers.

Of the gratitude and loyalty of the colored boys let me give an instance. When we were behind the lines, a private, whom all considered spineless and good-for-nothing, was severely reprimanded at two inspections for the condition of his rifle. After the second inspection was over an officer came up to him and pointed out in a friendly way how he could get the rust out of that shocking barrel. A week later they were in the trenches, a heavy barrage was bursting all along the parapet, and it became necessary for this officer to run through and find how an outlying position was making out. He stood outside the dugout and called for a volunteer to go with him, since, if he were hit, someone must carry the news to battalion headquarters. The men were clustered on the stairs and in the doorway. As the officer spoke, a shell nearly got him. For a moment no one moved. He called again, and the despised soldier whom he had befriended wriggled through the crowd in the doorway and rushed forward.

Many of them are deeply religious. The censors know this well from their letters. They have been spared, they say, and they thank God for it. It is a long, hard trail, but Jesus Christ will see them through. I remember well our old mess-sergeant, a very dark Negro, his close-curled hair shot with white, often coming up to me in quiet times, placing his hand on my shoulder and talking to me of the goodness of God in sparing us through the horrors we had seen. Indeed, God has been good to us. Through the years before us, may all who have been in that fiery furnace remember that they always represent the dead who lie in Flanders fields and work with strength and vision.

Colored soldiers are splendid "hikers." They have fine endurance, with a sunny disposition that keeps them from complaining. When a man falls out from fatigue or illness, their sense of humor asserts itself. Among white troops passing the sufferer, there would generally be muttered comments of sympathy on having been sent to France to be marched to death. The colored soldier who falls out, however, receives no mercy. Every man in line feels that he has proved himself a better walker than the unfortunate, and struts along the road, jollying his footsore comrade as he passes. Watch the change as the column, marching at route step, swings into some small French town where children and an old woman or two observe the passing army. The command of "Attention!" is not necessary. Every man swings into step, shoulders are thrown back, and extra distances between ranks close automatically. *Some one is watching them.* There was one comedian who stowed somewhere about him for these occasions a battered silk hat. We let him wear it — in small towns! The inhabitants stared at him and laughed. He was happy and made the whole company happy.

In their drilling they are like sensitive plates, responding to the tone of the officer in charge. No troops will do well under a slipshod drillmaster, but the colored man will deteriorate and become slack more quickly than the white. He responds immediately, however, to snappy commands and a soldierly appearance. He will snap through the manual of arms and march perfectly in close-order drill, with a slight, irresistible swagger. Let a superior officer come out to see such an exhibition as machine guns going into action in competition and they will tear down the field as if the guns they carried weighed nothing. They will almost burst their hearts with exertion, happy all the time because they are observed.

The colored soldier is generally a splendid physical specimen, with great powers of endurance. He is tireless, cheerful, and loyal and will follow like a dog through artillery barrage and the wind of machine-gun bullets. On the other hand, he has an extraordinary nervousness, does not like the dark, and lacks will and initiative. This last appears most clearly in the case of non-commissioned officers. Many will handle their men very creditably behind the lines, while to an officer some of them are full of intelligent suggestions (too full, if encouraged!). In hard conditions, however, the best of them, though showing no apparent fear, seem to be struck dumb. They do what they are told but move as if bewildered. I think they lack the free, independent spirit that stirs in the breast of the white; that rises within him when the shells are falling thick and says, "I am a better man than any ——— Boche, and I am coming through." Of course, you find the same spirit in some Negroes, but it is rare. They are boys. They do not grow up, even under shell-fire.

If I were to join the army again, I should like to serve with colored troops. They are so cheerful and willing, and they march so well. They enjoy the theatrical effect of their drill. They are extremely good with animals. Have you ever seen eight black boys hustling a wary old mule up into a freight car? All eight are clustered round his stern, lifting, pushing, shouting, laughing, while the mule braces all four feet on the sloping gang-plank. They do not fear his kicking, and in a moment the most obstinate of brutes is safe aboard.

Among themselves they are full of humor, tolerant, and kindly. The officer who, while with them, would not grow young again is indeed a slave to dull care. What a simple lovable people are these dark-skinned brothers of ours!

If I were to go fighting again, I should like to serve with them, too; but it must be realized that this is a very different proposition. I should like to have the power to raise a body of Negro troops. They should be picked men, and then picked again. To get noncommissioned officers for a company those of a battalion would be combed over, and these sergeants and corporals, when chosen, would be under close observation. In fighting qualities the average of the colored race is not as high as that of the white; but given the picked men and their thrice-picked leaders, with officers who understand their weakness and their strength, the result would be a body of troops that would shed great glory on their race. They should have a gradual training in war: that is, they would hardly be the men to throw into a terrific encounter as their baptism under fire. Such was to some extent the experience of the colored regiment with which I served. They had the advantage of a long training in the trenches before they took part in a big attack. They came through with a fine record. And let me say, with pride in the officers with whom it was my privilege to be associated, that they were well led.

I have said nothing about colored officers, because I have not known them; but this much I think is true: black still turns naturally to white for leadership, just as on the Southern plantation the slave turned questioning eyes to the planter. All the more credit to the colored officers, many of whom have led their men well.

Men of the South who face the race question bitterly and men of the North who wash your hands of it remember that races develop slowly! A few years ago these men were slaves in the cotton fields. A few years before that they were children in the jungles of Africa. They are children still. The race question is a topic far beyond the scope of this paper; yet, in considering it, let the white citizen remember the lovely traits of his colored brother. We have so much in power, prestige, and development which they have not. We inherit an independent spark, fostered through ages of war and upward groping. Let us hold out our hands and open our hearts to these wonderful boys who move among us, remembering that white and black lie side by side in the fields "over there."

INROADS ON CIVIL LIBERTIES

31   *Reinhold Niebuhr*
The Failure of German-Americanism

*The author describes the problems of "hyphenate" citizens in terms of
the largest such group, the German-Americans, who were especially sus-
pect during the period of World War I. Many of them experienced suspicion and harassment.*

Having believed ourselves to be one people, cemented by a
common love of our nation and bound by the power of new
ideals and liberties, we suddenly find ourselves broken into racial
groups whose old-world loyalties seem more powerful than their
new allegiance. We have found, to our sorrow, that our melting-
pot has not been able to undo in decades what the processes of
centuries had wrought on the hard metal of racial consciousness.
The result is that America is facing the problem of the "hyphen."
. . . With this problem on our hands, it is natural that larger
alien groups should engage our particular attention, and that
their doubtful loyalty, or divided allegiance, should especially
arouse our indignation. No group is larger than that of the
German-Americans, and those which are as large have the advantage of a closer relationship with us in language and customs.

SOURCE. Reinhold Niebuhr, "The Failure of German-Americanism," *Atlantic
Monthly* (1916), **118**:13–18. Reprinted from *The Atlantic Monthly*, Boston,
Mass.

The result is that the problem of the "hyphen" has centered in German-Americanism. . . . Whether the resentment that has been aroused against German-Americanism has been justified or not, the attention which it has gained has been inevitable. Having become a more or less tangible entity among the elements of our national life, it invites examination of its characteristics, if it does not justify criticism.

Such an examination must cover not only the present activities and tendencies of German-Americanism but its attitude toward American affairs and problems in the past. History ought to have a voice in determining whether present accusations of disloyalty are justified or not.

. . . a nation needs and demands the loyalty of its citizens, not only when its existence is at stake or when its claims upon their allegiance are put with particular force by the crises of physical combat. In times of peace also it requires their loyalty — their loyalty to its ideals, and their allegiance to the principles upon which it has been founded. Of the immigrant it is entitled to expect that he will place the virtues and powers with which his particular race has endowed him in the service of the ideals that animate the people with whom he has allied himself.

The German-American appears to have failed to meet either side of this obligation. He has been too often not only indifferent to our ideals but untrue to the virtues of his race. This is a charge that can easily be made against any immigrant; but since no immigrant came to our shores more richly endowed with the characteristics of a unique civilization than the German immigrant the charge seems to be particularly applicable to him.

The German-American has made contributions to our national life, but they have been economic rather than spiritual. He has served the body of our nation well, but his contribution to its soul-life seems to have been inadequate. In developing our national resources, particularly the agricultural resources of the Middle West, the German-American has had no inconspicuous part. His thrift and industry are proverbial, and these virtues were employed to good advantage upon our countrysides and prairies. . . .

German-Americanism has manifested a lack of interest in our political problems. German-Americans have played no prominent role in our political struggles. The Irish-American element, for instance, has been a far more potent factor in our political history. This does not mean that German-Americans ought to have acted as a racial group in our political struggles. Their purpose to do so now is one of the causes of hostility toward them. America wanted no political activity from them of a factional and selfish character, but it might have expected them to dedicate their knowledge of European affairs to the service of this nation. . . .

In the social development of the nation and in the agitation of social questions the German-American has been equally inconspicuous. We have, for the past years, been in the throes of a social revolution, or social reformation, which has given a new meaning to many of the old ethical conceptions. . . . In this tendency of our national life, however, the German-American has had no part. Like most men whose affluence was gained by industry and thrift, he is prone to attribute all poverty to indolence and to hold the individual completely responsible for his own welfare. Perhaps the fact that he has been engaged in agricultural rather than in industrial pursuits is an additional cause for his indifference to our social problems, which have so largely centered in our industrial and commercial life. At any rate, he has shown this indifference — and that in spite of the fact that he comes from a country that has been a clinic for the world in the methods of humanizing industry. . . .

In the development of the religious life of this nation the German-American has manifested an even more regrettable aloofness. Christianity has, without doubt, received a unique development in this country. Conditions have been particularly favorable for the solution of some of the old, vexing problems of Christendom. The problem of denominationalism is one of these. Nowhere in the world have different denominations and sects had such large opportunities to come in close contact with each other as in this country. Here they are all represented, and the spirit of fraternity, so dependent upon the consciousness of equality, is not jeopardized by special government privileges to some. This condition encourages them to emphasize those points of doctrine and polity on which they can agree and to minimize the points which still separate them. The result is that a spirit of fraternity has developed here which bids fair to culminate, at some time, into an organic and vital interdenominationalism.

In this development the German-American church has had no part. Among strongly denominational churches it takes first rank. It has maintained a studied, and sometimes a hostile, aloofness toward all interdenominational movements. Not even the more liberal of the German-American churches have entered very heartily into Christian fellowship with other churches. This unfraternal spirit is not a racial characteristic of the German but seems to be a surviving relic of the eighteenth-century orthodoxy of the German church. . . .

One other characteristic of organized German-Americanism deserves special mention. It is its opposition to all temperance reforms. If there is any activity which German-Americanism has undertaken as a unit, and which has brought it as a body to the attention of the American people, it is this opposition to the temperance movement, particularly the prohibition movement, in America. If German-Americanism was discredited in any way even before this war, it was because of its attitude upon this question. Next to the interests directly affected, German-Americanism has been the strongest opponent of prohibition in this country. The German press is particularly unanimously opposed to any and every kind of prohibition, and the German pulpit has given the opposition a less unanimous but even more effective support. Resentment against this attitude has grown with the phenomenal increase in prohibition sentiment among the American people.

The prohibition movement has come to express the most enlightened conscience of the American people. It has the practically unanimous support of the churches and is being championed with increasing vigor by the press. It is natural that opposition to a movement that has the support of the intelligent public opinion of our country should cause resentment, especially when it comes from a group of otherwise respected and respectable citizens. In this attitude, as well as in his attitude upon other issues, the indifference and hostility of the German-American to our ideals is a betrayal of the ideals of his own people. . . . We see upon every hand that, where the German-American is hostile or indifferent to our ideals, he is, in some sense, false to his own. It is difficult to find an adequate reason for this peculiar situation in which German-Americanism is found. Perhaps it is due to the fact that German immigration was largely drawn from the peasant class of Germany, which is ignorant of, and unaffected by, the influences of the modern German university, which has had such a large part in moulding contemporary German civilization. Perhaps it is caused by the fact that the German exodus to this country had virtually stopped before the modern Germany was born. Thus the attempt of German-Americans to remain true to the customs and conceptions of the fatherland causes them to perpetuate customs and ideals long since discarded in Germany itself.

Whatever may be the cause of the failure of German-Americanism, its failure is obvious. And this failure may be a contributory cause not only of the lack of esteem in which German-Americanism is now held in this country but also of the lack of understanding between Germany and this nation. This want of understanding may be only very indirectly responsible for the present ill feeling between the two countries. This seems rather to be due to more specific historical incidents. But the position of German-Americanism in this country would have been fortified against suspicions of disloyalty, and its defense of the German cause would have been more convincing and effective had it been less indifferent to the ideals and principles of this nation and more true to its own.

32   *Sarka B. Hrbkova*
Bunk in Americanization

The writer criticizes violations of civil liberty perpetrated by partici-
pants in "Americanization" crusades—efforts to eliminate indications of
ethnic origin such as language and customs—which were often aimed at
minority groups. These "Americanization" campaigns struck at the
much-praised concept of cultural pluralism. The Bohemian-Americans
discussed in the article stemmed from a nationality group within the
Austro-Hungarian Empire which favored the Allied cause.

It is inconceivable to the army of "Americanizers" who are
abroad in the land "seeking whom they may devour" why the
"alien" (anyone who speaks another language instead of English
or even in addition to English is so classified by the professional
"Americanizer") refuses to be melted and moulded instanter into
the pattern all duly described in the handbook issued by the
particular organization said "Americanizer" is representing.

Today practically every national organization in the United
States, religious, social, industrial, economic and political has
incorporated an Americanization department in its sphere of
activities. Their combined funds to be spent for "Americanization programs" runs up into the tens of millions. Then
there are hundreds of other organizations of State or local
significance which have undertaken the same ambitious program.

Out of this feverish and fanatical rush of first aiders to the
injured, it cannot be said that any one organization has clearly
defined a national ideal of what is really meant by Americanism. In all fairness to the leading men and women in the above
mentioned organizations it must be said that some of them

SOURCE. Sarka B. Hrbkova, " 'Bunk' in Americanization," *Forum* (1920), **63**:
428–439.

actually have in mind an ideal of what they would like to attain as far as the immigrant element is concerned. Unfortunately, however, their assistants, subassistants and minor "field-workers" —those who have the actual contact with the individual immigrant have, as a rule, a most chaotic and hazy notion of the *quod erat demonstrandum,* and their flounderings only serve to roil the waters all the more.

"57 VARIETIES" OF "AMERICANIZATION"

As a matter of fact "Americanization" does not mean the same thing to any two organizations engaged in their self-appointed tasks. To certain of them it means merely the naturalization and attainment of citizenship by the foreigners. To others it means the acceptance of a certain veneer or brand of religion along with the "dose." Some have a broad conception inclusive of every virtue under the sun. Another class, chiefly those heading large industrial establishments, regards Americanization as a fight for radicalism and bolshevism and often linked with it are quasi-foreign or so-called interracial organizations which purport to be friendly to the foreign-born in advising them, in highly paid advertisements in the foreign language press, not to take part in strikes or protests against economic injustice, though the latter term is never used, for obvious reasons.

The "57 varieties" of Americanization programs proposed by national, state or local organizations in more or less incoherent or general terms which sound big and inflatedly Fourth-of-Julyish involve the expenditure of millions of good American dollars. From such an investment one should reasonably expect some results. The "outward visible signs" of the immense outlay consist of probably 50,000 jobs for as many persons who just two years ago had never heard of "Americanization" and didn't know or care a rap about the immigrant or his troubles or our problems in having him in the United States. But today—avaunt! they are full-fledged "Americanizers" and glibly discuss at Mrs. Astorbilt's luncheon or at a prayer meeting of the Pink Teatotallers how they are implanting "American ideals" in the lowly foreigner and his more lowly wife. . . .

THE LAST REFUGE OF FAILURE

Americans are quick at adaptation—too quick sometimes, one meditates—and readily adjust themselves to the needs of the moment. In a sense Americans are opportunists if not always for pecuniary reasons then for their real desire to be of service. But unfortunately all the Minute Men who sprang to the "aid of their country" when the wave of Americanization first began to sweep over the country were not actuated by purely patriotic zeal or armed with the weapons of real understanding. A member of the California Commission on Immigration and Housing, which, by the way, very emphatically eschews the use of the word "Americanization" in connection with its very real services, which are only incidentally patriotic and never offensively or too obviously of that character, said recently, "The trouble is that every one who has failed at everything else thinks he's exactly cut out to do Americanization work." It is a fact that one of the men appointed as a regional director of American-ization with about eight States under his direction confessed to the writer that he had no idea what Americanization was nor had he ever had dealings with the foreign born, let alone de-voting even an hour's study to their needs or problems. Yet he jumped at the chance to be "Regional Director of American-ization" and would as soon have thought of cutting off his own nose as to refuse the appointment. No American ever admits his lack of fitness for a job. Versatility or the assumption of it is a truly American characteristic. That the bluff succeds frequently does not make it any the less a bluff. . . .

THE REAL "ALIEN ENEMIES"

The indiscriminate "bunching" of all foreign-born peoples with the disloyal element among the Germans has aroused the resentment of great groups of non-German and non-Magyar origin who unhesitatingly and faithfully supported the United

States Government when it most needed that moral and substantial backing.

Somehow the public has lost sight of the fact that it was not the Slav or Italic element in our population that betrayed the United States' cause, but that it was members of the Teutonic and Hungarian groups who failed in their support of the American cause. Moreover, the "traitors" in our time of stress were not foreigners unacquainted with English but English-speaking American citizens of Teuton origin.

During the war it was fully understandable that measures should be taken to suppress an enemy language but the extension of the prohibition to the languages spoken by our Allies in the world struggle is establishing a precedent unheard of even in Berlin. A prominent Iowa lawyer, in discussing the drastic measures of Governor Harding, writes: "We of Czecho-Slovak blood were good enough for America during the war to support the government with our lives and our fortunes, but, before the struggle overseas is fairly won, we are ignobly classed with our enemies and the language in which we all did faithful American propaganda service is suppressed." A woman who worked indefatigably for American war relief in Nebraska states: "Nebraskans refused to differentiate between the friendly and the enemy nations. This morning my aged mother who has knitted industriously for the Red Cross thoughout the war but who can speak only the Bohemian language was roughly treated by some extremists of native birth for using the Czech (Bohemian) language in speaking over the telephone to me."

The Siman language law passed early in 1919 by the legislature of Nebraska, while aimed ostensibly at the German parochial schools, wiped out temporarily instruction in every language except English. A decision of the Supreme Court handed down in December 1919 is to the effect that all instruction in public, parochial and denominational schools must be given in the English language up to and including the eighth grade, but permits people who send their children to the American public schools to provide for them foreign-language instruction in Saturday, Sunday or vacation schools outside of public school hours. This decision saves the day for Nebraska, which thus provides its rising generation with a thorough education in the

English language but does not deprive it of the advantage and opportunity of instruction in other languages as well. . . .

AN INTELLIGENT AND PATRIOTIC CITIZENRY

The spirit of America finds an echo in the heart of every Czecho-Slovak and in them it will find an intelligent and patriotic citizenry. It is the practice of certain Americans and not the principle of Americanism that is objectionable to the residents of foreign stock. It is all very beautiful for the native-born to rant in high-sounding phrases of the principles of freedom, equality and justice which our country supports, but it is rather disillusioning to read, in the news columns of every paper, article after article telling of political graft and crookedness, business profiteering and industrial wrongs. The effect of the chauvinistic editorial is refuted by the proof of actual daily occurrences and experiences. . . .

The excellent schooling facilities in Bohemia, which are justly a cause for pride to the Czechs, have given the members of that group unusual opportunities for social expansion. Among the immigrants over fourteen years of age who knocked at our gates, in the last score of years, the Czechs have an average of only a small fraction over one per cent of illiterates as against the Germans with about six per cent of illiterates and Magyars and North Italians with twelve per cent.

Since 1899, or in the last twenty years, 141,669 Czechs and 480,286 Slovaks have immigrated to America. The majority of the Czechs belong to the older and settled immigrants for they go chiefly to the agricultural states. They have become citizens and bear their burden of the responsibilities of the communities where they live equally with the native born. Admiration for the free institutions of this government has ever characterized them, and because they are inveterate readers and active in community work they have kept abreast of the spirit of the times. But they cannot understand why, after being Americans for a generation or more, they are now to be "Americanized."

33   *Must We Go to Jail?*

After the United States entered the war Congress passed legislation that placed severe restraints on newspapers and magazines and led to outraged complaints that it had infringed on the freedom of the press.

The Espionage Act approved by the President on June 15 provided that any publication "containing any matter advocating or urging treason, insurrection or forcible resistance to any law of the United States is hereby declared to be nonmailable." Very good! "Treason," as we reiterated last month, "must be made odious," by all available means. But now comes a supplementary provision in the Trading with the Enemy Act, approved on October 6, to the effect that "it shall be unlawful for any person, firm, corporation, or association, to transport, carry, or otherwise publish or distribute any matter which is made nonmailable" by the Espionage Act under penalty of $500 fine or of imprisonment for a year or of both.

What does this mean? Penalties can still be exacted, we suppose, only after convictions by courts of law, but it is within the province of the Postmaster General to pronounce a periodical "nonmailable" and to ruin it by stopping its publication and distribution pending appeal and trial. The *World* calls this "a species of lynch law," of which "the Postmaster General is judge, jury and executioner"—an opinion shared apparently by Mr. Burleson himself, who spoke to the correspondent of the *Evening Post* as follows:

"I realize that it is a great power, but I intend to be as conservative and as cautious as it is humanly possible to be. There isn't going to be any injustice done. No truly loyal American has anything to fear. And I want to state right now that the purpose of this legislation is not to prevent criticism of the Government

SOURCE: "Must We Go to Jail?" *North American Review* (1917), **206:**673–677.

or the Administration or the Post Office Department. It is not
aimed against Socialist publications or any other kind of publications as a class. The newspapers can denounce me or the Administration all they like, and they can have such criticism circulated
through the mails. But if we find newspapers preaching disloyalty, newspapers that are really German at heart and in
secret sympathy with the German Government which we are
fighting, newspapers which are trying to make the masses in this
country believe that this is a capitalists' war and that the Government therefore ought not to be supported—those publications we
intend to suppress with a firm hand. Because we are at war with
the Imperial German Government. The country has declared
war. Anyone who deliberately sets afoot a propaganda to dis-
courage support to the Government as against its enemies is
doing a treasonable thing. We must win the war, and we cannot
brook disloyalty at home."

That is to say, having "a giant's strength," he would not be
"tyrannous" in using it—a consoling reassurance no doubt, but
hardly satisfying. Of course, we "cannot brook disloyalty at
home" nor can we countenance "preaching disloyalty," but how
precisely and with certainty to determine whether one is "really
German *at heart*" or "*in secret* sympathy" with the enemy is past
our imagining. However, following the Cabinet meeting, Mr.
Burleson spoke more explicitly.

"We shall take great care not to let criticism which is personally
or politically offensive to the Administration affect our action,"
he said. "But if newspapers go so far as to impugn the motives of
the Government and thus encourage insubordination, they will
be dealt with severely.

"For instance, papers may not say that the Government is
controlled by Wall Street or munition manufacturers or any
other special interests. Publications of any news calculated to
urge the people to violate law would be considered grounds for
drastic action. We will not tolerate campaigns against conscription, enlistments, sale of securities, or revenue collections.
We will not permit the publication or circulation of anything
hampering the war's prosecution or attacking improperly our
Allies."

Mr. Burleson explained that the policy of the foreign language newspapers would be judged by their past utterances and not by newly announced intentions.

"We have files of these papers, and whether we license them or not depends on our inspection of the files," he said. German language newspapers not licensed will be required to publish English translations.

Mr. Burleson said no Socialist paper would be barred from the mails unless it contained treasonable or seditious matter.

"The trouble," he added, "is that most Socialist papers do contain this matter."

Even the faithful Springfield *Republican* finds this disturbing —and we cannot wonder. "If," it remarks, "Mr. Burleson is going to suppress all publications that venture to 'impugn the motives of the Government' he must in the end virtually suppress all hostile criticism of the Administration and destroy free speech in this country.". . .

Readers of the *Review* need not be informed that at the very outset of the war we urged the establishment of a wise and capable censorship which should be wholly independent of the working departments and should form a valuable connecting link between President and people; but, the suggestion having been rejected, as betwen Messrs. Daniels and Baker, originally designated, and Mr. Burleson, now duly installed, we hesitate to express a preference. Upon the whole, we are disposed to lean tactfully towards the latter, for the quite practical reason that it is he who wields the axe. It is only a question of time when this *Review* will be stopped and we shall be sent as far along the road to jail as the courts will permit: we perceive that plainly enough. Not that we shall say anything which could possibly be regarded as "personally or politically offensive to the Administration"; nothing like that; Heaven knows we are scrupulously and invariably polite, although frankly in view of prospective judgment upon "past utterances," we should feel relieved to be assured that certain back numbers of this journal have been mislaid. But when it comes to telling us that we must not express an opinion, if such we should happen to hold, respecting undue influencing of the Government by "Wall Street," by "munitions makers" or by "any other special interests," the betting will cease instantly. And when the Postmaster General notifies us, as quoted by the *Republican* that "there is a limit"— for a public journal—"and that limit is reached when it begins to say that this Government got in the war wrong," we respond in kind that the limit is not even in sight. In point of fact—preserve us, good Lord!—this Government *did* get in the war wrong; it ought to have been better prepared. But we have never talked about that and would not now if we were not goaded to it. We hasten, nevertheless, to inform our prospective executioner that one Theodore Roosevelt has been making remarks along that line for some time and is aching to go somewhere, preferably to France, but why not to jail? He would make a glorious martyr.

The solemn truth is that this legislation, interjected surreptitiously as it was, is wicked, vicious, tyrannous and ought never to have been enacted. We beg merely in conclusion, and in friendliness, to suggest to the Postmaster General that he study carefully the First Amendment to the Constitution of the United States and reflect gravely upon the fate which befel John Adams when he undertook to impose *his* notion of sedition upon a nation of freemen jealous of their liberties and capable of maintaining them.

34   The Case of the Columbia Professors

*Shortly after the United States entered the war Columbia University
dismissed two faculty members for alleged seditious statements. The
result was an academic cause célèbre, which raised the question of minority rights, particularly freedom of thought and expression, in a particularly striking manner. The* Nation, *critical of Columbia's action, considered that it was representative of comparable inroads on academic
freedom occurring at other institutions of higher education during the
same period.*

It is now perfectly plain that the American Association of
University Professors has vital work cut out for it. The dismissal
of Professor Cattell and of Assistant Professor Dana from Columbia University raises an issue of such far-reaching importance
that the real facts in the case should promptly be laid before the
public, after the most careful study. We are quite aware that
the metropolitan journals have barked a chorus of satisfaction
at these dismissals. Echoing Secretary McAdoo's recent threat in
Cleveland that every pacifist shall be silenced and suppressed,
these newspapers are determined that the United States shall be
less tolerant of the minority, however impotent, than England or
Germany. But the facts in these cases are not clear; there is
even a suggestion that the authorities have been not altogether
ingenuous in the presentation of facts. On top of this came protests from three such strong members of the faculty as Messrs.
John Dewey, Beard, and Robinson, and now Professor Beard
resigns because he will no longer stay on a faculty dominated
by trustees "who have no standing in the world of education, who
are reactionary and visionless in politics, narrow and mediæval
in religion." Professor Dewey declares the action of the trustees

SOURCE. "The Case of the Columbia Professors," *Nation* (October 11, 1917),
105:388–389.

to be "degrading." Plainly, we have here not only a great
academic sensation, but the need for more light. No more important university issue has yet been raised in America.

We are aware of the difficulties involved in the personalities of
the two dismissed professors. If Mr. Dana has said half the things
attributed to him by hostile reporters, he is lacking in discretion,
to say the least. As for Professor Cattell, he has admittedly long
been a thorn in President Butler's side. But granting that they
are known as "difficult characters to deal with," the question still
is what have they done to merit their explusion? Were they
really guilty of sedition, or merely bad taste, or were they, in
the exercise of their undoubted right to their own political
opinions, sacrificed to the spirit of intolerance which has been
so amazing a phenomenon of our entering the world war on behalf of democracy and democratic ideals? Professor Cattell declares that he did not urge that our troops should not be sent to
France, but only that conscientious objectors to war should be
kept at home. Where does the truth lie? Obviously, some third
party ought to establish the facts. Columbia must not object if
the trustees' position is viewed with skepticism when it recalls
the hasty action they took in constituting an inquisition into
professional views last spring only to beat an equally hasty
retreat when the faculty showed fight—it was currently reported
that an entire section would have walked out had the trustees
persisted.

This Columbia episode is of all the greater importance because
we Americans have been dwelling with such just reprobation
upon certain German efforts to suppress the minority opinion
there, and because there are other cases to cause genuine concern
for academic freedom here at home. Thus a professor in the
University of Minnesota has been ousted for his war views by
the Board of Regents—on order of the State Defence Council of
Minnesota, a body which has been sufficiently autocratic and
overbearing to please the Kaiser. The University of Nebraska's
faculty has been similarly assailed by the Defence Council in its
State, and at present there is a great deal of pressure being
brought to bear upon still another Western university for the
dismissal of a teacher whose sole offence is that he attended the
meeting of the People's Council in Chicago. He took no part in

the proceedings—which, by the way, must have been legal, however they may have seemed unwise or ill-timed, since not a single arrest was made by the hordes of secret-service agents, city detectives, militia, etc., who thronged Chicago for the express purpose of arresting anybody who in the slightest degree transgressed the law. But the mere fact of his presence in Chicago is now made the ground for demanding this teacher's removal, although not one in twenty of the protestants, it is safe to say, has the remotest idea what the People's Council's programme was, what it was really striving for, and whether it was loyal or not. Incidentally, it may be added that one must go far back in American journalism to find another instance of such flagrantly malicious reporting as vented itself upon this ill-fated and ill-managed convention.

Obviously, the question of these professors merges into the general question as to what right the minority has to be heard in war-time. We have not learned that any of them are guilty of disloyalty or that they have deliberately tried to impede the Government's carrying on of the war. But like the Christian Pacifists—a group of clergymen and church-workers, without any political motives—whose peace meeting in *a private house* in Pasadena was violently broken up last week by uniformed Home Guards, just as antislavery meetings were dispersed seventy years ago contrary to all law and decency, so today American professors who would treat of the war contrary to prevailing opinion do so at their peril. They cannot be restricted to a given area like Bertrand Russell; dismissal is the one penalty, whether the offence be great or small. And it is just because the right to free speech must be upheld, throughout the country, that these professorial cases become so important.

If freedom of legitimate criticism is denied within college walls as it may be denied in Congress—it will not be safe anywhere. If councils of defence can order the removal of professors they dislike, why should chambers of commerce, merchants' associations, and the commercial travellers' societies hesitate to lay down what they think should be taught in war or in peace? A precedent like the one established in Minnesota is so far-reaching and so ominous as to call for a new and rigid definition to the rights of a teacher to express himself in times of stress and for the utmost resistance if the case in point proves to be an indefensible as is affirmed. As matters stand now, if another James Russell Lowell were to compose another "Biglow Papers," he would probably be denied the mails in case he went so far as to repeat the famous line, "And ez for war I call it murder," and then be dismissed outright. For the sake of all concerned, the limits of academic freedom should be defined as soon as possible.

Americans surely do not wish to be as illiberal and intolerant as the Prussians, to whose abominable philosophy and criminal war actions every honest American, be he pacifist or militarist, is absolutely opposed. For instance, Professor F. G. Nicolai, of the University of Berlin, a convinced pacifist, was deprived of his rank in the medical reserve corps because of his views and was severely criticized for refusing to sign that disgraceful statement of the 93 German professors which dealt so terrible a blow to the standing of German universities and their teachers. He opposed this document and the prevailing trend in Berlin, and, together with Professor Albert Einstein and Privy Councillor Wilhelm Forster, circulated—without success—one of a totally different character. In Professor Forster's case he has been so openly outspoken against the war and the war policies of the Kaiser as to have been boycotted by all his associates, many of whom signed a petition asking for his removal. He is said to be living in Switzerland.

Shall it be said of the United States, the champion of democracy, that its academic authorities are going to be equally unwise and ungenerous in this war to carry democracy to Germany?

35   *John Lord O'Brien*
             Uncle Sam's Spy Policies

One of the special assistants to the Attorney General explains the policies of the Department of Justice regarding freedom of thought and expression during the war emergency and warmly defends the agency against its detractors.

With the perspective of years no achievement of the Americans in the war will loom larger or more significant than the triumph of American civil law, the lack of internal disorder and the law-respecting attitude observed throughout the country by both citizen and alien alike. No other nation came through the struggle with so little disorder and with so little interference with the civil liberty of the individual. No historical appraisement will leave out of its reckoning consideration of the attitude of Attorney-General Gregory and the Department of Justice. There is no other department of the Government whose activities during the war have more nearly affected the life and habits of the citizen; none has been so fully responsible for the protection of the constitutional and civil rights of the citizen—and, it may be added in passing, no other department has received such a plenitude of advice from the citizen.

Early in the war certain principles were definitely decided upon. Those principles were adhered to by the Department of Justice throughout the war, and the policy formulated at the beginning remained unchanged to the end. This policy was based upon the confidence felt in the law-abiding character of our citizens and the conviction that in this country it was very generally recognized that liberty meant obedience to law, self-

SOURCE. John Lord O'Brien, "Uncle Sam's Spy Policies: Safeguarding American Liberty During the War," *Forum* (1919), **61**:407–416.

control and self-restraint, and that in every part of the country the strongest deterrent influence against disloyalty was neighborhood public opinion.

It was the view of the department, therefore, that there should be no repression of political agitation unless of a character directly affecting the safety of the state; that the constitutional guarantees protecting life and property must be strictly enforced, and that under no circumstances should the military or naval authorities be permitted to do any act which would arbitrarily interfere with the life and habits of the individual citizens. And, further, that protection of the innocent was at all times a correlative duty with punishment of the guilty. . . .

MAINTAINING AMERICAN FAIR-PLAY

There was no community in the country so small that it did not produce a complaint because of failure to intern or execute at least one alleged German spy. These instances are cited, not to make light of the danger of hostile activities, nor to imply that incessant vigilance was not necessary in watching the German activities, but to show how impossible it was to check that kind of war hysteria which found expression in impatience with the civil courts and the oft-recurring and false statement that this Government showed undue leniency toward enemies within our gates.

In no field was this temper more evident than in the attitude created by these unofficial organizations toward unnaturalized Germans and Austro-Hungarians throughout the country. Early in the war these people were naturally regarded by the public as our largest potential element of danger. The expression, "enemy alien," used in the old Internment Statute of 1798 to describe these unnaturalized residents, in and of itself carried the impression of hostility to this country. Thousands of intelligent citizens and some important newspapers continually advocated the internment indiscriminately of all alien enemies; and no amount of statistics on their loyalty or of good conduct on the part of this large class of persons seemed to have the effect of lessening the agitation. They were under suspicion by the ma-

jority of their neighbors in every community; they were the subject of incessant investigation at the hands of police officials and
amateur detectives, and the extent to which their normal lives
were interfered with can only be a matter of conjecture.

No other policy so clearly and sharply differentiates America
from the other nations at war as the attitude which it took on
the subject of interning enemy aliens. It was a policy not fully
understood and, in the earlier period, was freely criticized; but
I venture to say that of all the policies advanced by this Government in the war no other pays a higher tribute to the American
ideal of justice, and I believe that the verdict of the future upon
this policy will be one of unconditional commendation. For, in
a time of war, while punishing offenders severely, we found it
possible to close our ears to insensate clamor and to perpetuate
the American standards of fair play. . . .

AMATEUR DETECTIVES MAKE OUTRAGEOUS WRONGS

Although the Attorney General, so far as was possible, employed his powers to secure the protection of civil liberties,
nearly all cases where outrages were committed against individuals lay outside the scope of Federal jurisdiction. During the
various Liberty Loan drives, the campaigns for war charities
and the loyalty drives, many complaints of ill-treatment and
coercion were received by the Attorney General from people
against whom assessments had been levied by nonlegal bodies
who fixed and collected subscription quotas. Considering the extent of the country and the extremely patriotic temper of the
people, it is perhaps remarkable that great injustice was not done.
Nevertheless, some of the instances reported, isolated as they
were, were cases of outrageous wrong for which no relief could
be afforded by the Federal Government.

Owing to local conditions of intensive patriotism and the fact
that those wronged were often aliens or persons under a cloud
of supposed disloyalty, it was difficult for them to secure redress
at the hands of their local authorities. The one large outstanding fact which most affected the enforcement of law throughout
the war was that the public looked upon the war as the nation's

affair and not only laymen but the local law officials looked to Washington for the fighting of all wrongs whether they were disloyal utterances, hostile activities or overzealous patriotic activities. Taken by and large, the number of cases of seriously wronged individuals was negligible; but at that, the number was too large.

It is too early to appraise the work of local councils of defense and it would be wrong to attempt to do so by mere generalization. The differences between them were almost as many as the number of the organizations. In connection with floating war loans and decrying disloyal sentiments they performed services of immeasurable value. On the other hand, representing as they did the most intense spirit of local patriotism, they interfered with the civil rights of many people, and evidences were not wanting that in occasional cases their interference with civil rights and civil liberties resulted in serious wrongs. The very fact of their being in existence made them listening posts for rumormongers as well as for legitimate complaint. For example, one Federal officer of the Middle West recently informed the writer that he had received approximately three thousand complaints from local councils of defense in his territory out of which less than one hundred were worthy of serious attention. Some of them provoked grave discontent, the effects of which cannot now be estimated, because of the manner in which, without legal authority, they arbitrarily assessed, against members of their respective communities, demand quotas for Liberty Loans, Red Cross and other war charities. . . .

MAINTAINING CIVIL RIGHTS

The general policy of the Attorney General toward free speech has been well understood and adhered to by his subordinates with a good deal of consistency. From the outset, recognizing that free expression of public opinion is the life of the nation, we have endeavored to impress upon our subordinates the necessity for keeping within the lines of policy established by Congress and bearing in mind at all times the constitutional guarantees. Repeatedly their attention has been called to the fact that expression of private or public opinion relating to matters of governmental policy or of a political character must not be confused with wilful attempts to interfere with our conduct of the war. At all times we have had before us the dangers which follow attempts to restrain public discussion and, so far as instructions issued by the Attorney General have been concerned, they have consistently and at all times emphasized this general policy.

No full discussion of the subject of civil liberty could be had without giving consideration to the powers exercised by the Post Office Department in connection with printed matter alleged to be of a character in violation of the Espionage Act. These powers of the Postmaster General were exercised by him alone; the Department of Justice had no share or part in administering them, and for that reason no discussion is here made of that field of war control.

The attitude of the Attorney General opposing the suggestion of military courts is a matter of common knowledge. That suggestion, in the light of subsequent events, now appears grotesque. Not only have we been opposed to any such idea, but our policy lay deeper. We were opposed to all and any interference on the part of the military or naval authorities with the civil rights and even the habits of the average citizen. Behind the scenes we took frequent occasion to emphasize this view which, I may add, was thoroughly approved by the Secretaries of War and Navy, respectively.

PART THREE

Peacemaking, 1919–1920

Unless all the right-thinking nations of the world are going to concert their purpose and their power, this treaty is not worth the paper it is written on because it is a treaty where peace rests on the right of the weak, and only the power of the strong can maintain the right of the weak. If we as a nation indeed mean what we have always said, that we are the champions of human right, now is the time when we shall be brought to the test, the acid test, as to whether we mean what we said or not. PRESIDENT WOODROW WILSON, *September* 1919.

TREATY DEBATE

36   *William E. Borah*
        Militarism in a League of Nations?

The Progressive but isolationist Senator from Idaho advances his argument against membership in the League of Nations, stressing in particular its alleged militaristic attributes and its introduction of "evil old-world forces" into American life. Internationalism is equated with Prussianism as subversive of traditional Americanism.

At the time that the League to Enforce Peace was first organized in Philadelphia in 1918 it was apparent to those who gave it consideration that it must rest ultimately upon force, upon the principle of repression. Naturally, the first question was, "How are you going to raise your army to sustain this vast military program or this league based upon force?" Would the citizens of the United States volunteer to enter the army for the purpose, for instance, of settling difficulties in the Balkans? Would the American boys leave their homes or the farms or the factories for the purpose of taking part in the adjustment of a controversy between Japan and Russia over Manchuria? How are you to have a sufficient force in a free nation with which to maintain the program outlined by this league? . . .

We shall never be able to call into activity or into service a

SOURCE. William E. Borah, "Militarism in a League of Nations?" *Forum* (1919), **61**:297–306.

sufficient force from the American homes to do our part in a
league of nations—to settle the controversies of Europe and of
Asia by means of military power, except by fastening conscription upon the American people. At a time when other Governments, which have had experience with conscription, are pledging the people that it shall be abrogated and eliminated from
their system this Republic is to have it made permanent. While
others are trying to get away from it the League to Enforce Peace
would require that we ingraft it upon our system as an abiding
principle. Lloyd-George and others who have spoken upon the
subject have said that it shall not only be eliminated, but that
it shall be forgotten as a precedent. The League to Enforce
Peace states that the basis upon which it expects to operate is
that of inaugurating this principle even in time of peace. That
is the practical, and the first practical, proposition with which
we shall have to do in the organizing of this particular form of
a league. . . .

After the war has come to an end, with our enemies defeated
and all the great naval powers friendlier than ever before in our
history, we propose to spend $600,000,000 in the next three years
upon a powerful fighting machine. Is this not a direct challenge
to the good faith of our allies, or does it not throw doubt upon
the sincerity of our own professions? Above all, is it not a signal
act of injustice to the people of this country, who have paid
taxes and bought Liberty Bonds and saved and stinted and
denied themselves in this crisis? Is the American taxpayer to
have no place whatever in this program of national affairs save
that of a coddled peon? Are we going on with this shameless
orgy of expenditure until the people are forced to cry out with
the voice of revolution against the madness that is grinding
them to powder? The expenditures of this war will amount to
easily thirty billions, and yet we are proposing to add billions
upon billions for war purposes in time of peace. . . .

[T]he views of the ex-President, the platform of the league,
the constructions placed upon the platform by its authors and
by those who are in sympathy with it, here is what the League to
Enforce Peace proposes: Conscription in time of peace and a
large standing army; the greatest navy in the world; adding by
the navy alone to our great tax burdens from two hundred and

fifty to three hundred million dollars a year; the transferring, if not legally, in effect, the power to declare war from the Congress of the United States to some tribunal over which the people themselves, who must fight the battles and pay the taxes, have no control; the renouncing of the doctrine of Washington and the entering of the politics and alliances of Europe; becoming a member of a league from which we cannot withdraw; the abandonment of the Monroe Doctrine and permitting Europe to interfere in the affairs of the Western Continent; the sending of American soldiers to Europe and Asia and Africa whenever any disturbance arises, although it may not affect our people at all; and the whole scheme has just one ultimate power and that is military force—the same power and the same principle which every despot has relied upon in his efforts against the people when the people were seeking greater liberty and greater freedom, the same power which George III and Wilhelm II made the basis of their infamous designs. That is the program to be given to the American people under the soporific term of a league to enforce peace.

ARE WE YIELDING TO EVIL OLD-WORLD FORCES?

The fact is we have come in contact with two evil forces from the Old World—Prussianism and internationalism. Instead of repelling and rejecting them we are yielding to their slimy maw the proudest heritage ever left to the keeping of any people— American principles and the American conception of government. One's two hands are not more alike than, in the last analysis, are the doctrines of Lenin and Trotsky and that of Wilhelm and Ludendorff. Both contemplate world dominion and the utter destruction of the national spirit everywhere. Each would undermine and destroy the individuality of all governments and compound all under the universal rule. Both are founded upon treachery, deceit, lying, repression, force, decimation, and assassination. They came together at Brest as naturally and as inevitably as common criminals combine to stay the hand of the law. They were both against America and everything for which America stands. But while civilization starts back in shuddering contemplation of the rule of either, certain American statesmen propose to take something from the creed of both and substitute it for the teachings of Washington and the faith of millions of American homes. Instead of our own government, controlled and directed by the intelligence and patriotism of our own people, instead of American standards and American principles, instead of devotion to our institutions and to our own flag, we are to have an international superstate resting upon Prussian force, with a vast army of repression, a superstate in which the national spirit stands rebuked and the international flag is the sole symbol of our hopes. I do not know what the future has in store.

God pity the ideals of this Republic if they shall have no defenders save the gathered scum of the nations organized into a conglomerate international police force, ordered hither and thither by the most heterogeneous and irresponsible body or court that even confused or confounded the natural instincts and noble passions of a people. Let us leave these things—the lives of our people, the liberty of our whole nation—in the keeping and under the control of those people who have brought this Republic to its present place of prestige and power. What we need in this hour is faith in the institutions that our fathers gave us, faith in the career which everything indicates we shall enjoy unless we in public place prove recreant to our duties in this great trying hour.

37   *Franklin H. Giddings*
              Our Mythological History

The writer, an historian, calls for a new presentation and interpreta-
tion of American history in accord with the facts and needs of a world
undergoing massive change. He is especially hopeful of eliminating mis-
leading national myths by refusing to perpetuate them as legitimate
historical truths. He takes direct issue with the general outlook on the
American past espoused by leaders such as Senator Borah.

The fact that true American history has not been taught in
our schools need not be confusing to our patriotism or our national pride. It will be necessary to change many of the historical statements contained in our textbooks of American history
as they are now used in American schools.

The modifications of American history should not be confusing, because its facts in the present vision of world affairs have
become merely the horizon of world democracy. In the glory of
its National evolution American history became a Western
World mythology. It consists of a series of war dramas and
political conflicts associated with the names of Washington,
Monroe, Jefferson. These men, of that hour in historical time
when they were leaders, have become the gods of American mythology. Since mythological events are symbols of human ideas,
they may well enough be retained, but in their proportionate
values. . . .

It is the intention of American educators who are devoting
themselves to teaching Americanism to America to readjust the
proportion of historical nationalism so that it will apply to the
new conditions of world democracy. We must create a dynamic
patriotism. The first impression which the children of this

SOURCE. Franklin H. Giddings, "Our Mythological History," *Forum* (1918),
60:333–339.

generation must receive of American history requires a new vision. It must no longer consist on the one hand of a dry record of dates and statistics nor on the other hand be taught as a fanciful fairy tale of a nation sufficient unto itself and independent of world evolution.

American history, as it is being taught in our schools, reflects our national character in the adornment of mythological splendor. Our chief historical facts are heightened by the influences of a great ideal—Liberty.

But Liberty, let us recognize, in the form and figure in which America has pictured her is no longer a symbol of isolated Americanism. She is the Goddess of the world's ambition, she does not represent a unique ambition, peculiar only to American freedom. She does not belong exclusively to America. Although freedom was the first impulse behind the events of American history, Liberty is no longer the supreme Goddess of the Western Hemisphere only.

The emotional thrill which Liberty inspires through the record of the facts of our American history has been enormously extended. We are discovering that Liberty has represented not only our national independence but also our international safety. Our world vision has been an error, because we are not independent of world evolution. . . .

We are given the impression in American history, and no doubt it was the chief impulse of our National birthright, that the Western Hemisphere should become a paradise sufficiently remote from the long reach of Imperialism to remain an Eden. In the enjoyment of that idea we were impressed with its wisdom. For that idea our ancestors fought bitterly and brilliantly to establish an isolated continent, where Liberty in ornate and poetic splendor, should preside. It did. These errors of American history in this period of our national career become obvious to us today when we realize that there is no such thing as human isolation for individual or for nation. . . .

The chosen theme of American history, namely the achievement of national isolation, can no longer remain its basis. If we look at the actual historical facts in their trite relations to modern international facts, the American Revolution was not confined to America. It was the first phase of a world movement. It was by no means a war against the English people. It was not a war of English men in America against English men in England. It was a war of the liberal element of both countries against aggressions of a German crown. This has not been explained in American history. Mythology has dealt with symbols and not with broad facts.

American history is glorious enough without distorting its actual events. It is glorious enough to be recorded in all its realism. We cannot detract from the glory of Washington or of Jefferson by placing them in their true proportion to world events. Nor can we detract from the Declaration of Independence when we show that it was only a first blooming of Revolutionary thought. It is our duty to place American history in the true perspective of world history, otherwise it cannot be adequately taught. The rise of democracy must be explained and that can only be done through a complete understanding of the ambitions of autocracy. . . .

It never dawned upon our nation that we had a world mission. We were content to be an object lesson to the world. We were proud of our isolation, we were united in the idea that we could work out our own salvation, giving a free pattern of national ideals to other countries. Scarcely five years ago not a man in America could have believed that we should have a million soldiers in France today fighting to make the world safe for democracy.

We must accept the situation and change our history. Our old security has gone. The United States has suffered disillusion. We have learned that no country can be independent of the civilization that surrounds it. Either the American idea or the Prussian idea must survive. One or the other must make room. It has taken American invention to destroy the mythology of American history, the aeroplane and the submarine. The sea has ceased to protect us, and both the sea and the air have become routes for invasion.

The time for the patriotism of isolation has gone; we need rational patriotism in organization and service and to be conscious of a world situation. American history must be moulded to this idea.

Instead of a narrow nationalism, we have a new sentiment of

national force called Americanism. It is a living, growing thing. It is something more than personal liberty. It is charged with ideas of freedom and of equality of opportunity, and it opposes coercion and conquest. It has become a passion to preserve these ideas at any cost. Of course, it is related to the old Americanism which worked out the present destiny of America. Where before Americanism represented a mythological fairyland of free isolation, it is today charged with a world mission. We can no longer shout "America for Americans." We will no longer be content with a false sense of security. Not until all the people of the earth are guaranteed equal freedom to work out their destiny will America have achieved her place in the sun.

RADICALISM AND THE RED SCARE

38   *Annie Pike Greenwood*
Letters from a Sage-Brush Farm

The author discusses the motivations behind the organization and activities of the Non-Partisan League and draws attention in particular to the profiteering of distributors ("middlemen") and the errors of the federal government.

MY DEAR SISTER,

So Bert, having been a farmer himself before you married him, would like to know something about the Non-Partisan League. Well, I suppose I should be satisfied that I have roused some interest in at least one of your family. Maybe, if he is interested, you will be; but since he has become owner of an electric-power plant, I suppose we can't hope for his support at election time in case the Non-Partisans should get a footing in Utah. And yet I don't see why not, because he is just a little independent owner, and he may butt his head against one of the power trusts before he gets through, just as we farmers are butting ours against the water trust and the power trust here in Idaho.

All we farmers paid our sixteen dollars to join the League when the organizers came around. At the primaries we outvoted both Democrats and Republicans. But at election we fell way

SOURCE. Annie Pike Greenwood, "Letters from a Sage-Brush Farm," *Atlantic Monthly*, 124:310–321. Reprinted from *The Atlantic Monthly*, Boston, Mass.

behind. You see, Frank Gooding wanted to be United States Senator, and he spent over a thousand dollars a day in newspaper publicity trying to convince the farmers that the League leaders were unpatriotic—I.W.W.'s in disguise. Charges of disloyalty were made against our leader, Townley; and of course, a good many concluded that there must be smoke where there was fire. . . .

So you see, Bert, what we are up against. I can see you chuckling to yourself, and congratulating yourself on your wisdom in leaving that plough in the middle of the field when you made your declaration of independence to your father. I, too, would quit, but my fighting blood is up, and if I get out now it would be with a sense of defeat. Thank God, I have at last found a cause worth fighting for, though like all other Great Causes of the world's history, the people whom I would see most benefited seem the most indifferent. I hope it is not sacrilegious when I say I know how Christ felt when he was trying to save the people of the world in spite of their indifference. But the farmers will wake up. I will not sink under this injustice, and I will not rise, unless all farmers rise with me.

Of course, we shall have to suffer. We have had to suffer being pioneers on a pioneer farm, and we shall have to suffer being pioneers in this new political party. There are times when I feel that I am of the blood of martyrs, and other times when I would almost sell the whole cause for a real porcelain bathtub! But even Christ had his temptation. . . .

Why doesn't our good old government ask us farmers what we want, instead of assuming that superior paternal attitude, as much as to say, "You farmers are all little children. We know what is best for you. Just be good and do what we tell you, and by working hard some day you can have a few dollars in your old age—oh, not much; but you won't need much, because we shall teach you how to live all these years on so little that you can get along on very little when old age grips you.". . . Were our crops a failure? Quite the contrary: we had good crops considering the insufficient water distribution with which we had to contend, and we thought we were going to be on Easy Street every year for six years. Didn't we have enough land? One hundred and sixty acres ought to be enough. Where is the trouble? The lack of market and marketing facilities, and the middle-man. The men who have handled our crops have grown rich.

I am not a Socialist. I am not dreamer enough for that. But my beloved government is taking the wrong course with us farm people. Let the government supply us with middle-men instead of county agents—government-paid middle-men who would have no object in profiteering on us. Let the government supply us with warehouses to store our surplus—every year a part of our good money goes to build granaries which stand idle half the year, and I board the builders of the granaries. Let the government find out where our crops should go and see to the shipping of them, so that we who have plenty can supply those who want. Let the government study our conditions, cost of production—including farm-labor, husband's labor, wife's labor—and set the price on crops accordingly, different in each locality, and we shall all be glad to abide by the results and the consumer will not suffer, there being no middle-man to pay. . . .

I am not ever going to write such a letter as this again. But I am boiling over. I have stood all that I am going to, in silence. I am not a successful farm-woman. I love the farm, would rather live on it than any other place in the world, but I am not willing to accept silently the wrongs of the farm life. Like Wolsey if I had served any other profession as faithfully as I have served that of being a farmer's wife during the past six years, I should now be independently prosperous.

Well, Bert, how do you like this *spiel?* Never mind, I am dead in earnest. I must stay with the babies, or, like Carrie Nation, I would get out and smash a few things. But I have a man that I am going to back to the utmost.

Here's yours, for the galvanized tub in the kitchen.

THE FARMER'S WIFE

39   *Carleton H. Parker*
                         The I.W.W.

The writer provides a sympathetic but objective analysis of the radical labor movement that encountered extensive persecution during World War I as a presumed fount of "Unamericanism." The public reaction in the United States against the International Workers of the World reflected a general wartime and postwar reaction against movements supposedly inspired by foreigners or foreign ideas.

The American I.W.W. is a neglected and lonely hobo worker, usually malnourished and in need of medical care. He is as far from being a scheming syndicalist, after the French model, as the imagination might conceive. His proved sabotage activities in the West total up a few hop kiln burnings. Compared to the widespread sabotage in prison industries, where a startlingly large percentage of materials is intentionally ruined, the I.W.W. performance is not worth mentioning. It is to the less romantic economic phases that we must turn for the true cost of the problem.

The characteristic of the I.W.W. movement most worthy of serious consideration is the decay of the ideals of thrift and industry. To this can be added, in place of the old-time traditional loyalty to the employer, a sustained antagonism to him. The casual laborer of the West drifts away from his job without reflection as to the effect of this on the welfare of the employer; he feels little interest in the quality of workmanship and is always not only a potential striker but ready to take up political or legal war against the employing class. This sullen hostility has been steadily growing in the last ten years. It is not as melodramatic as sabotage but vastly more important. To the

SOURCE. Carleton H. Parker, "The I.W.W.," *Atlantic Monthly* (1917), **120:** 651–662. Reprinted from *The Atlantic Monthly,* Boston, Mass.

student it is of major importance, because it can be linked up more directly and with more accuracy to its psychological causes. In a word, it is a natural psychic outcome of a distressing and antisocial labor condition. This sullen hostility develops very naturally the surface manifestations of unpatriotism, hostility to religion, and unlawful action; but the more important characteristic is the deeper economic one of the growing unreliability and decay of the workmanlike spirit among the migratory laborers. . . .

The I.W.W. is, as has been said, the aggressive American labor movement, emerging at the lower and less disciplined social level. The not surprising inability of the American citizen to note the growing class-consciousness of the trade-union movement made it certain that he would not read the writing on the wall regarding the strike methods, which would be manifest when this class struggle gained force and form among the migratory casual labor of the West. If the American trade-union world is only conditionally patriotic in its attitude toward the war, the I.W.W. is violently negative, for the same reasons, though they are more deeply felt. Casualties and deaths in the trenches, with their all-diverting suffering at home, will reinforce patriotism and silence for a time the class demands and cries; but the ingredients of the social mixture will not be changed to any important degree. . . .

It is fortunate for our analysis that the I.W.W. membership in the West is consistently of one type and one which has had a uniform economic experience. It is made up of migratory workers currently called hobo labor. The terms "hobo miner," "hobo lumberjack," and "blanket stiff" are familiar and necessary in accurate descriptions of Western labor conditions. Very few of these migratory workers have lived long enough in any one place to establish a legal residence and to vote, and they are also womanless. Only about ten per cent have been married, and these, for the most part, either have lost their wives or have deserted them. Many claim to be "working out," and expect eventually to return to their families. But examination usually discloses the fact that they have not sent money home recently or received letters. They are "floaters" in every social sense. Out of thirty suicides in the cheap lodging-houses in San Francisco in the month of December 1913 but two left behind any word as to their homes or their relatives. Half of these migratory workers are of American birth, the other half being largely made up of the newer immigrants from southeastern Europe....

It is a conventional economic truism that American industrialism is guaranteeing to some half of the forty millions of our industrial population a life of such limited happiness, of such restrictions on personal development, and of such misery and desolation when sickness or accident comes that we would be childish political scientists not to see that from such an environment little self-sacrificing love of country, little of ethics, little of gratitude could come. It is unfortunate that the scientific findings of our social condition must use words which sound strangely like the phraseology of the Socialists. This similarity, however, should logically be embarrassing to the critics of these findings, not to the scientists. Those who have investigated and studied the lower strata of American labor have long recognized the I.W.W. as purely a symptom of a certain distressing state of affairs. The casual migratory laborers are the finished product of an economic environment which seems cruelly efficient in turning out human beings modeled after all the standards which society abhors. The history of the migratory workers shows that, starting with the long hours and dreary winters of the farms they ran away from or the sour-smelling bunk-house in a coal village, through their character-debasing experience with the drifting "hire and fire" life in the industries, on to the vicious social and economic life of the winter unemployed, their training predetermined but one outcome and the environment produced its type.

The I.W.W. has importance only as an illustration of a stable American economic process. Its pitiful syndicalism, its street-corner opposition to the war, are the inconsequential trimmings. Its strike alone, faithful as it is to the American type, is an illuminating thing. The I.W.W., like the Grangers, the Knights of Labor, the Farmers' Alliance, the Progressive party, is but a phenomenon of revolt. The cure lies in taking care of its psychic antecedents; the stability of our Republic depends on the degree of courage and wisdom with which we move to the task.

40   *A. Mitchell Palmer*
The Case Against the "Reds"

A powerful reaction against "radicalism" in various forms swept the country immediately after the end of the war. One of the leading progenitors and sponsors of the "Red Scare" was the Attorney General of the United States, who summarizes his fears of Bolshevism and his methods of extirpating it.

In this brief review of the work which the Department of Justice has undertaken, to tear out the radical seeds that have entangled American ideas in their poisonous theories, I desire not merely to explain what the real menace of communism is, but also to tell how we have been compelled to clean up the country almost unaided by any virile legislation. Though I have not been embarrassed by political opposition, I have been materially delayed because the present sweeping processes of arrests and deportation of seditious aliens should have been vigorously pushed by Congress last spring. The failure of this is a matter of record in the Congressional files.

The anxiety of that period in our responsibility when Congress, ignoring the seriousness of these vast organizations that were plotting to overthrow the Government, failed to act, has passed. The time came when it was obviously hopeless to expect the hearty cooperation of Congress in the only way to stamp out these seditious societies in their open defiance of law by various forms of propaganda.

Like a prairie-fire, the blaze of revolution was sweeping over every American institution of law and order a year ago. It was eating its way into the homes of the American workmen, its sharp tongues of revolutionary heat were licking the altars of

SOURCE. A Mitchell Palmer, "The Case Against the 'Reds,'" *Forum* (1920), 63:173–185.

the churches, leaping into the belfry of the school bell, crawling into the sacred corners of American homes, seeking to replace marriage vows with libertine laws, burning up the foundations of society.

Robbery, not war, is the ideal of communism. This has been demonstrated in Russia, Germany, and in America. As a foe, the anarchist is fearless of his own life, for his creed is a fanticism that admits no respect of any other creed. Obviously it is the creed of any criminal mind, which reasons always from motives impossible to clean thought. Crime is the degenerate factor in society.

Upon these two basic certainties, first that the "Reds" were criminal aliens and secondly that the American Government must prevent crime, it was decided that there could be no nice distinctions drawn between the theoretical ideals of the radicals and their actual violations of our national laws. An assassin may have brilliant intellectuality, he may be able to excuse his murder or robbery with fine oratory, but any theory which excuses crime is not wanted in America. This is no place for the criminal to flourish, nor will he do so so long as the rights of common citizenship can be exerted to prevent him.

OUR GOVERNMENT IN JEOPARDY

It has always been plain to me that when American citizens unite upon any national issue they are generally right, but it is sometimes difficult to make the issue clear to them. If the Department of Justice could succeed in attracting the attention of our optimistic citizens to the issue of internal revolution in this country, we felt sure there would be no revolution. The Government was in jeopardy; our private information of what was being done by the organization known as the Communist Party of America, with headquarters in Chicago, of what was being done by the Communist Internationale under their manifesto planned at Moscow last March by Trotzky, Lenin and others addressed "To the Proletariats of All Countries," of what strides the Communist Labor Party was making, removed all doubt. In this conclusion we did not ignore the definite standards of personal liberty, of free speech, which is the very temperament and heart of the people. The evidence was examined with the utmost care, with a personal leaning toward freedom of thought and word on all questions.

The whole mass of evidence, accumulated from all parts of the country, was scrupulously scanned, not merely for the written or spoken differences of viewpoint as to the Government of the United States, but, in spite of these things, to see if the hostile declarations might not be sincere in their announced motive to improve our social order. There was no hope of such a thing.

By stealing, murder and lies, Bolshevism has looted Russia not only of its material strength but of its moral force. A small clique of outcasts from the East Side of New York has attempted this, with what success we all know. Because a disreputable alien —Leon Bronstein, the man who now calls himself Trotzky—can inaugurate a reign of terror from his throne room in the Kremlin, because this lowest of all types known to New York can sleep in the Czar's bed, while hundreds of thousands in Russia are without food or shelter, should Americans be swayed by such doctrines?

Such a question, it would seem, should receive but one answer from America.

My information showed that communism in this country was an organization of thousands of aliens who were direct allies of Trotzky. Aliens of the same misshapen caste of mind and indecencies of character, and it showed that they were making the same glittering promises of lawlessness, of criminal autocracy to Americans, that they had made to the Russian peasants. How the Department of Justice discovered upwards of 60,000 of these organized agitators of the Trotzky doctrine in the United States is the confidential information upon which the Government is now sweeping the nation clean of such alien filth. . . .

WILL DEPORTATION CHECK BOLSHEVISM?

Behind, and underneath, my own determination to drive from our midst the agents of Bolshevism with increasing vigor and with greater speed, until there are no more of them left among us, so long as I have the responsible duty of that task, I have discovered the hysterical methods of these revolutionary humans with increasing amazement and suspicion. In the confused information that sometimes reaches the people they are compelled to ask questions which involve the reasons for my acts against the "Reds." I have been asked, for instance, to what extent deportation will check radicalism in this country. Why not ask what will become of the United States Government if these alien radicals are permitted to carry out the principles of the Communist Party as embodied in its so-called laws, aims and regulations?

There wouldn't be any such thing left. In place of the United States Government we should have the horror and terrorism of bolsheviki tyranny such as is destroying Russia now. Every scrap of radical literature demands the overthrow of our existing government. All of it demands obedience to the instincts of criminal minds, that is, to the lower appetites, material and moral. The whole purpose of communism appears to be a mass formation of the criminals of the world to overthrow the decencies of private life, to usurp property that they have not earned, to disrupt the present order of life regardless of health, sex or religious rights. By a literature that promises the wildest dreams of such low aspirations, that can occur to only the criminal minds, communism distorts our social law. . . .

It has been inferred by the "Reds" that the United States Government, by arresting and deporting them, is returning to the autocracy of Czardom, adopting the system that created the severity of Siberian banishment. My reply to such charges is that in our determination to maintain our government we are treating our alien enemies with extreme consideration. To deny them the privilege of remaining in a country which they have openly deplored as an unenlightened community, unfit for those who prefer the privileges of Bolshevism, should be no hardship. It strikes me as an odd form of reasoning that these Russian Bolsheviks who extol the Bolshevik rule should be so unwilling to return to Russia. The nationality of most of the alien "Reds" is Russian and German. There is almost no other nationality represented among them.

It has been impossible in so short a space to review the entire menace of the internal revolution in this country as I know it, but this may serve to arouse the American citizen to its reality, its danger, and the great need of united effort to stamp it out, under our feet, if needs be. It is being done. The Department of Justice will pursue the attack of these "Reds" upon the Government of the United States with vigilance, and no alien, advocating the overthrow of existing law and order in this country, shall escape arrest and prompt deportation.

It is my belief that while they have stirred discontent in our midst, while they have caused irritating strikes, and while they have infected our social ideas with the disease of their own minds and their unclean morals we can get rid of them! and not until we have done so shall we have removed the menace of Bolshevism for good.

RETURN TO NORMALCY

41   *Harry Emerson Fosdick*
The Trenches and the Church at Home

A well-known preacher considers the effect of the war on the churches of the country, in particular as they would be evaluated by the returning soldiers and sailors. To Fosdick the war experience seemed to validate the theories associated with the term "social gospel." The impact of the war ensured that the churches could not return to "business as usual."

Everyone must realize that the churches cannot possibly come out of this war in the same state in which they entered it. Nothing is going through this fire without becoming malleable or, becoming malleable, can resist the pressure of remoulding circumstance. And the men of the army will wield an enormous influence on all the changes. . . .

[O]nly a shallow observer can suppose that these men are really as boyish as they appear. In this experience they are going down to the heart of life. They have faced a cause that asked of them their all and they have made the great decision. Death, that skillful discriminator between things transient and things eternal, is their constant companion. . . .

The best among them have been initiated by this war into an insight that neither books nor schools nor threescore years

SOURCE. Harry E. Fosdick, "The Trenches and the Church at Home," *Atlantic Monthly* (1919), **123**:22–33. Reprinted from *The Atlantic Monthly*, Boston, Mass.

of civil life can give any man. And the pith of the result is this: they have been where only the elemental needs of men are real, where only the fundamental faiths and virtues matter, and they swiftly divine the essential from the accident. They have a quick instinct for what is genuine, for what rings true and really counts. Above all, they hate ineffectiveness and make-believe and unreal talk. And what they hate they have no patience with; they have learned to fight; they are not tolerant. Woe to the man who even now in France addresses them with unctuous phrase or convential doctrine or wordy exhortation! He will lose his audience and speak to vacant seats before he has well begun.

And these men, by millions, are soon coming home!

That glorious, ominous fact the churches seriously must face. We Christians in America have been asking ourselves, ever since this war began, what we could do for the boys in France. We need now to face another question: what are these returning soldiers going to do to the churches in America?

So far as I can see from months of living with the army, there are some things in the churches' life on which the hostility of the soldiers especially will fall. For one thing, how intolerable to those who have caught the devotion of the army is a certain habitual selfishness in the churches' appeal to men! If in France today, in speaking to the soldiers, anyone suggests that perhaps they soon will die, that if they do they may go to hell unless they are "prepared," and that therefore they had better believe something religious to avoid the sad contingency, that man incontinently shuts up, or else he leaves France, or more probably he does both. The soldiers will not listen to him; the army will not tolerate him. The reason is not simply that playing on morbid fears is an assault on the army's morale: a deeper reason makes this all too familiar appeal of the churches unendurable. There is a fundamental antipathy between such talk and the spirit in which the whole army is living. The former is thoroughly self-centered. The latter is gloriously self-forgetful. . . .

The churches for generations have been urging upon us an individualistic and self-centered gospel. We have been continuously supplied, in hymns, in liturgies, in sermons, with Jonathan Edwards's dominant ideal, "I make seeking my salvation the main business of my life." Even when this self-regarding motive has not been centred on a *post-morten* heaven, it has been centred quite as selfishly on this present life. God, a gigantic policeman, forever clubbing those who break his traffic regulations and feeding with goodies from his ample pockets those who mind his word, so that one had better keep upon his kindly side — H. G. Wells is not the only one who was brought up in the churches on that kind of deity. . . .

Against the background of the millions of self-forgetful men who fought in France, how dark this record looks! Many a soul is being saved there. Many men, returning, will bless America with a heft and range of character that they did not have before. But they did not go to France to save their souls. They forgot themselves and went to France to save the world. They are learning that innermost salvation that never comes except through social sacrifice; they have found their lives by losing them in a cause. In the midst of them one feels furiously the shame of the selfishness with which the churches often angle after men. . . .

When the returning soldiers open their assizes, another indictment will undoubtedly be pressed against the church: the pettiness of her sectarian emphases. From the days of the prophets until now, august souls in religion have tried to make first things stand first, and to save the church from her arch sin of "specializing in irrelevancies." And in our generation the belated futility of our denominations, the shame of our stress on dead issues and our negligence of live ones, has been so obvious, that scores of voices have been lifted in agitated protest. But still our churches, for the most part, have jogged on their complacent way. Circumferential trivialities have become the business of the churches. The intellectual classes, trying to think real thoughts about live issues, have gradually drifted away, until Christianity faces today, in the defection of the universities, not from religion but from the churches, a crisis of the first magnitude. . . .

We of the churches, in our pleasant day-dreams, love to picture Zion calling the evil world to righteousness. It is a shocking experience therefore to discover that our most virile manhood strenuously objects to our whole idea of what righteousness is. The soldiers seriously think that the character which the churches seek consists of little more than abstinence from a multitude of pleasurable things. In the midst of a tremendous generation, when men are rising to superhuman heights of positive character in service of gigantic aims, the churches often stand, in the imagination of the soldiers, insisting on a list of prohibitions, which the army as a whole regards with sheer contempt; thinks it narrow, negative, piffling; passes it up as unworthy of a real man's ambition to observe. . . .

A sergeant of the British Regulars, seeing gas-patients die — twenty-four hours of drowning agony — exclaimed to a friend, "This sort of thing makes me want to suffer everything for everyone once and get it over!" Consider such a man going home to hear some dominie, who never came within sight of so vital a Calvary, urging through a whole sermon the sin of baseball on Sunday afternoon. Is this overdrawn? Yet it is a picture that hangs in the minds of the soldiers. They honestly think that the ethical interest of the churches chiefly centres in just such questions of abstinence.

These soldiers see ahead of them a generation facing prodigious problems, on whose successful solution the weal of humanity depends. They see arising questions of international organization and of social justice, which, unanswered, will make defeat out of the most splendid victory that they can win. They see the need of great character directed to great ends. They do not want to die in vain. They want a fairer, more fraternal world to show for their travail. But only vaguely, if at all, do they associate the churches with that deep desire or rely on them to help much in achieving it. The churches which they have known have impressed multitudes of them as having no ethical enthusiasm for anything except negative ideals of individual behavior. And one returns from France vehemently feeling that, in the midst of so great a generation, to be a small man or a small church obsessed by piddling prohibitions is disgrace. . . .

Comradeship is the glory of the army, and in that comradeship previous wealth, rank, occupation do not count. Only manhood matters. I do not see how these soldiers are coming home to many of our churches, where pews are owned or rented, and where the congregation is so seated that a man's relative income can be estimated by his comparative distance from the altar of the Lord's sacrifice. The class-divisions in our churches are in ill accord with the democracy of the army. There is a shocking incongruity between an attack at the front — rich and poor, learned and ignorant, prominent and obscure, going over the top together — and a congregation in a wealthy metropolitan church singing —

"Onward Christian soldiers, marching as to war."

As one considers these accusations which the spirit of the army brings against the churches — the selfishness of our appeal, the pettiness of our sectarian emphases, the negativeness of our ethic, the undemocratic quality of our fellowship — he sees that they are no theoretical complaints. They fall upon us all in vital spots. Some, in this last generation, were for saving the churches by keeping them theologically and ritually orthodox; some were for saving them by making them liberal; and now the army drags up the manhood of America where we can talk with it — and behold! the soldiers do not know much about our points of controversy, take little stock in any of them, waste no time to think or wind to talk of them, but seem to feel that, liberal or orthodox, our churches may incontinently be consigned to oblivion unless they can make some vital changes in their *life*. . . .

42   *Jacob Gould Schurman*
       New Ideals of Social Progress

The President of Cornell University inveighs against the excesses of radicalism but calls for a rejection of balance-of-power statecraft and national isolation, arguing that the outcome of the Great War had transformed the realities of international politics.

Here in the United States we shall soon be celebrating the tercentenary of the landing of the *Mayflower*. It is a time, therefore, for a revival of those ideals of democracy, liberty, and justice which have made our American republics what they are. The spirit of the new age must not be reaction, and still less revolution, but reform and progress. The cure for Bolshevism, whether in Europe or America, is not Bourbonism but the bettering of opportunities for the struggling masses and the removal of the evils which might alienate them from our existing form of constitutional democracy and drive them out into the wilderness to worship the false gods of sovietism, communism and anarchy. . . .

Let us trust the sound sense of the American people. Let us meet the folly and errors of the fanatics with the all-conquering weapons of fact and reason. If the Bolsheviks rule Russia by force and murder, let America, now as heretofore, govern herself by free discussion and enlightened public opinion and the deliberate vote of the majority. Our laws must of course be enforced and sedition rigorously put down. But America cannot save her soul by stifling free thought and inquiry or by deporting arkloads of alien revolutionists or denying constitutional right to radical and even mischievous citizens and parties.

SOURCE. Jacob Gould Schurman, "New Ideals of Social Progress: Our National Destiny Is Pre-Eminently in the New World," *Forum* (1920), **63**:315–324.

GREED AND GRAB GAME OBSOLETE

The old international system with its partial alliances, its bullying of the weak, its game of greed and grab, will no longer satisfy the plain people in all lands who have dreamt that this war should end war and who have been inspired by their faith and ideals. If their hope is balked, then Russia will not be the only country in which the fountains of the political deep overflow and overwhelm existing institutions with a revolutionary flood.

In the reorganization of international relations, which is now the great question before the world, the choice must be between alternative policies. It is impossible to have the advantages of both policies and the drawbacks of neither. The nations may continue as in the past to live each their own sovereign life with occasional and temporary alliances, as expediency may dictate, with other sovereign states but bearing the responsibility only of their own individual interests, with little or no regard for the welfare of the society of nations as a whole and with no obligation to foresee and avert causes of misunderstanding, strife, and war as they may from time to time develop in and through the interaction of these rival, self-contained, and independent powers. That is the course which the nations of the world have followed during the latter centuries of human history. It is not, however, the only possible system of international relations or the only one which has ever been practiced. . . .

The result of the world war has shattered the German dream of world domination by force. But the organization of the nations of the world to promote common national interests and maintain peace may be attempted not by means of force and subjugation but by the voluntary union of free, independent, democratic nations. And if the yearning of the peoples of the world for friendly international relations and peace is not to be balked and disappointed, this is the course which must now be pursued.

COLLAPSE OF OLD INTERNATIONAL SYSTEM

I assert that the system of international relations under which we and our fathers have lived has broken down; that its collapse was due to the change of economic, commercial, financial, social and political conditions in the modern world; that any attempt to re-establish it will be rendered nugatory by the continued existence of these conditions; that the sound instinct of the plain people of the world in all nations yearns and clamors for a new and better world order; and that if this instinct is disregarded and over-ridden by statesmen the gravest consequences are certain to ensue.

The world cannot go back to the nineteenth century system of a European balance of power and the hermitary seclusion of America. How can the balance of power be re-established in Europe when Germany has been vanquished and when Russia and Austria-Hungary and Turkey have been disintegrated and resolved into their constituent parts and replaced by numerous independent nationalities? And how can America resume her ancient isolation after the war in which it has been demonstrated that, owing to new methods and means and instrumentalities of warfare, on land and sea and air, no great nation can probably ever again remain neutral but must, in defense of its interests and security and for the maintenance of law and justice, be inevitably drawn into the conflict whenever two or more great nations of the modern world resort to the dread arbitrament of war?

From the political point of view the principal result of the war has been the democratization of Europe. The kaiseristic and militaristic empire of Germany has gone; the military power of the Hapsburg dynasty is broken and the congeries of nationalities it forcibly held together have fallen asunder; the czaristic and autocratic empire of Russia has collapsed and no one knows how many independent nations may arise on its ruins; gone also is the power of the sultan, the Mohammedan associate of those recent Christian despots, and the ancient peoples of Syria, Palestine, Armenia, Arabia and Mesopotamia have shaken off the shackles of their terrible bondage.

But while democracy has gained immensely by the resolution of Europe into its original atoms of nationality, the risks of war have been greatly increased by this multiplication of independent nations. The territories of three or four great empires of the past are now dotted over with groups of embryo states. If we may judge from our own experience in America the next step in the process of their development will be by way of federation. If such a development occurs, however, it will be a matter of growth and time. Meanwhile these numerous states will exist as separate and individual political entities. America will be almost as much interested in the maintenance of peace among them as England or France. For America can never forget that it was an attack on a little country like Serbia which brought on the great cataclysm under the force of which the world has been reeling since 1914.

43   *Charles Evans Hughes*
Our After-War Dangers

The defeated Republican candidate for President in 1916, who was to become President Harding's Secretary of State, concerns himself in this article with the problems of what was soon to be called "normalcy." He favors decentralization of governmental power but centralization of private economic power, always assuming a proper degree of regulation in the public interest.

We emerge from the war with a new national consciousness; with a consciousness of power stimulated by extraordinary effort; with a consciousness of the possibility and potency of cooperation and endeavor to an extent previously undreamed of.

Gains like these should be abiding, for they mark not only

SOURCE. Charles Evans Hughes, "Our After-War Dangers: In Saving the World Have We Lost Our Republic?" *Forum* (1919), **61**:237–242.

increase of knowledge and the sharpening of the tools of the mind but an improvement in attitude and appreciation. The new vision is never lost. We are unworthy of our victory, if we look forward with timidity. This is the hour and power of light, not of darkness. We have not defeated an insensate ambition to become the victims of our own inability to govern ourselves. We have made the world safe for democracy, but democracy is not a phrase or a form, but a life, and what shall that life be?

Some anxiously ask, "What has become of our form of government?" In saving the world, have we lost our Republic? The astounding spectacle of centralized control which we have witnessed has confused many and turned the heads of some. But this, for the most part, has been the manifestation of the Republic in arms, fighting as a unit, with powers essential to self-preservation, which the Constitution not only did not deny but itself conferred. So far as we have harnessed our strength for war, we were acting under the Constitution and not in violation of it. But wherever, in the desire to take advantage of the situation for the purpose of fastening some new policy upon the country, there has been resort to arbitrary power through acts unjustified by real or substantial relation to a state of actual war, such acts will receive the condemnation they deserve when they are brought to the determination of the proper tribunals.

AN ABUSE OF FEDERAL POWER

With the ending of the war we find ourselves with the familiar constitutional privileges and restrictions, and it behooves officers of Government to realize that to make a pretense of military exigency·for ulterior purposes, when military necessity has ceased, is simply an abuse of power which will not be permitted to escape censure. It is undoubtedly true that whenever, during the War, extraordinary powers were fittingly exercised and Governmental control was assumed for war purposes, the readjustment to conditions of peace must of course be effected gradually and with the circumspection essential to the protection of all the public and private interests involved. But the immediate purpose should be to readjust as soon as may be, not to use war powers to control peace conditions, a proceeding essentially vicious and constituting the most serious offense against our institutions. What changes we shall desire to make in order to suit new conditions which follow the War we must make deliberately after discussion and with proper authorization. Power policies must be prosecuted with the authority and distribution of powers and according to the methods which pertain to peace. . . .

Along with this is the grave question of putting the direct operation of these great activities unnecessarily under political control. That is the most serious question. The dovetailing of Government with business is apt to injure both. Such is the havoc wrought by political machines, demanding that position and profit go with political favor and as political reward. We shall have quite enough of this sort of thing in the necessary extension of governmental activities without courting additional difficulties.

INEFFICIENCY THE BLIGHT OF PUBLIC UNDERTAKINGS

It is regrettable, but it is true, that governmental enterprise tends constantly to inefficiency. It would, from any point of view, be unsafe to take the experience of the last year as a guide. The splendid stimulus of the War Spirit put us at our best. The general disposition to serve and to be content made conditions exceptionally advantageous for governmental experiment. Again, the situation in the past year with respect to the movement of traffic has been abnormal. But, apart from these considerations, the experiment would not appear to afford a basis for expecting a net balance of benefits in government ownership and management. I do not mean to imply that the record of private enterprise is an agreeable one, but on a fair examination of conditions where governmental management has been maintained, I believe that from the standpoint of efficiency the comparison favors private enterprises and that in this country we cannot afford to ignore the fact that inefficiency is the blight upon our public undertakings. It cannot fail to be observed that even in connection with the War, despite the endeavor and patriotic impulse of countless workers, inefficiency in important fields of activity has been notorious. The notion that the conduct of business by Government tends to be efficient is a superstition cherished by those who either know nothing of Government or know nothing of business. The tendency is strongly the other way.

There is just as much danger to our prosperity in undue decentralization as in overcentralization. Take our railroads as an example. If we are not to have government ownership, we must have a sensible plan of regulation. We must have a plan of regulation which will permit sound credit and growth, which will stabilize securities and offer inducements for investment, while insuring adequate service at reasonable rates. The democracy saved by a world war ought to be able to supervise great undertakings in a fashion which will really serve the common interest. Regulation which does not promote efficiency is self-condemned; and with respect to interstate carriers, State lines are not economic lines. Congress should provide, as it has power to provide — aside from war powers — a comprehensive plan of regulation with relation to districts corresponding to the broad divisions of actual operations, and the entire field of the activities of interstate carriers should be covered appropriately by recognition of the interdependence of through and local rates and of the interblending of operations in the conduct of interstate and local business, so that in the exercise of the dominant power of Congress for the protection of interstate commerce all conflicting regulations would be avoided and the basis of efficiency secured.

HOW TO SAVE OUR PROSPERITY

But in endeavoring to escape the evils which are likely to attend upon government ownership and management, it is folly to go to the other extreme and to sacrifice the advantages and economy which cooperation in these activities may afford. Reasonable opportunity for concert under government supervision is necessary to afford the best service and prevent waste, and if we have learned this lesson from recent experiences it will be a great gain. . . .

We have had the experience of many years in trying to impose rules of uncertain scope with respect to restraint of trade. Lawyers have been unable to tell their clients whether proposed conduct would elicit the praise due to a conspicuous business success with corresponding gain to the community or would land them in jail. Of course we cannot go forth to win our proper place in the world's trade under such uncertainties and restrictions. And it is idle to talk of removing economic barriers abroad while maintaining them at home. In the first place, the mere size of a business does not warrant its condemnation. Mere size may carry the germs of dissolution, but if it means soundness of organization and economic strength we need it, provided there is proper supervision to prevent abuses. Wrong-doing, and not a mere conception of power, should be the basis of governmental restraint and prohibition. All power than can be used can be mischievous. If we aim at actual wrongs, we shall be more successful than if we attack bogies. Define and punish wrong, but free commerce from being hampered by fear of constructive evils.

Is it not entirely possible to maintain governmental supervision which will give reasonable opportunity for doing reasonable things instead of seeking to maintain rules of conduct which shackle American enterprise? Neither labor nor the general public gains anything from denying free scope to honest business, and to secure this legitimate freedom it should be the function of Government to provide intelligent supervision which will aim at the detection and punishment of abuses and not at the crippling of opportunities rightly used. . . .

HAVE WE THE HUN SPIRIT?

But whatever freedom it may have, American industry will not thrive unless it is instilled with the spirit of justice. We have fought this War to substitute reason for force. We love our Republic because it represents to us the promise of the rule of reason. There is no assurance of stability in industry if it is dominated by the selfish profiteer, or by men who regard human beings as mere economic units, or by men, whether employers or employees, who live with the ambition to be little Kaisers ruling by their little divine right, whether of wealth or of "pull" or of any position of power. If we are to establish peace within our own borders, we must cooperate to destroy the Hunnish spirit of tyranny wherever we find it.

There are no difficulties in the field of industry which cannot be solved if we insist on methods of justice. The whole international aim is to enthrone justice. How shall we hope to attain this end among the nations if we cannot establish justice in our own community?

44   *Anthony Caminetti*
Need We Fear Immigration?

The Commissioner General of Immigration seeks to quiet fears that the nation would be inundated by a great flood of immigrants from Europe in the wake of the war. He thought the war's aftermath might depress rather than stimulate an influx of foreigners. The article did not forestall an irresistible postwar movement toward restriction of immigration.

All prophecy right now can consist of little more than conjecture and by the nature of conditions must be largely futile. This is particularly true of prophecies as to immigration, for we do not know what the policies of governments, including our own, will be nor, more important still, what effect the war and its aftermath will have on the instincts and inclinations of those people who might be classed as potential immigrants to our country.

One would have thought naturally that many Europeans would have endeavored to escape the actual fires of war by emigrating to America or other countries far from the war zone. Of course shipping and other conditions made emigration difficult. However, it would seem that the war tended to depress rather than

SOURCE. Anthony Caminetti, "Need We Fear Immigration?" *Forum* (1919), 61:343–348.

to stimulate the instinct of migration among the peoples most vitally affected by the violence of the conflict.

Immigration to this country from Europe fell off tremendously as soon as the war began in 1914 and continued to decline more or less steadily until, during the fiscal year ending June 30, 1918, there was but little net gain in our population from that source. In fact during that year only 110,618 immigrant aliens entered the United States from all sources, while 94,585 immigrant aliens left the country during the same period. This left a net gain of less than 18,000.

The decade preceding the opening of the European war gave us annually an average immigration exceeding one million and the net increase in population from immigration sources in the fiscal year ending June 30, 1914, was 769,276.

WHAT INFLUENCES IMMIGRATION

Speaking broadly two considerations underlie nearly all alien immigrations:

1. Social conditions.
2. Economic conditions.

The first brought about the founding and original development of our country.

The second accounted largely for the phenomenal growth in population characterizing the last fifty years of our history and upon which was builded our modern-day industrial greatness.

Whatever changes the war will cause, it may be assumed that the migration of peoples will continue to be influenced as heretofore by social and economic conditions, barring, of course, artificial restraints or inducements.

Therefore immigration to the United States or emigration from the United States in coming years is apt to depend substantially on the social and economic conditions existing in this and those other countries whose citizens are admissible as immigrants.

SOCIAL IMPROVEMENTS ABROAD DUE TO THE WAR

It is probable that the war will produce great social improvements throughout most of Europe. The many reforms projected and the promise of land distribution to the masses in many countries where hitherto it has been held by the privileged few may retard the current that has been flowing towards us for generations; and yet, with all that, the average European is likely to continue to look upon our country as the great haven for freedom. And there is no doubt in my mind that many thousands will continue to seek refuge here for the same reasons, though they may not be so potent, as inspired the bulk of our early immigration.

Nothing but pure conjecture can be ventured as to the future operation of the other chief moving force in the tide of immigration, i.e., economic conditions.

If European countries maintain the validity of their war obligations, taxes will in future years demand a tribute which few persons until lately believed any people could bear. Those burdens may be reduced somewhat through lessened expenditures on military establishments, more economical governments and more equitable distribution of the taxes, but that they will be far beyond those of ante-bellum days, then considered highly oppressive, is certain.

Yet we must realize that the citizens of a number of European countries, England of course is included in this statement, bore, during the past four years, burdens far weightier than any they can expect for the future, and that those burdens were accompanied in some ways by a degree of individual prosperity among the masses exceeding any they had ever enjoyed in peace times. That such prosperity was economically false may be true; but the fact is that despite the tremendous tax of active war workmen in nearly all the countries involved enjoyed better wages, and more favorable wage margins, than they had been accustomed to.

While food conditions in Europe for the present are distressing and threaten much suffering, such is only a temporary or passing factor which will be removed as peace-time production gets under way.

We must remember also that the four years of war had great adverse effect on the populations of European countries. While emigration all but ceased, millions were killed or died from disease or wounds at the front, millions were incapacitated, millions of civilians died or were broken by the strains and privations of war, and the birth-rate dropped almost universally.

Then, also, it may be estimated that there is more work at hand in Europe for those who survive, or rather more work needing to be done, than was the case before. All the vast destruction of war calls, at least potentially, for replacement and the deficits in the implements of peace-time commerce caused by the deflection of energies into the activities of war need to be replenished. Indeed, the outlook for the European workingman of the peasant class, barring the period of adjustment from war to peace, may be much better than it was before the war.

Despite the tremendous destruction caused by the war and the huge debts incurred by the governments involved and the consequent possible increase in taxation, it is not extravagant to imagine a postwar Europe offering to the potential immigrant attractions superior to those he had prior to 1914.

It is also true that the experience of war intensified the love of most Europeans for their native lands and gave added potency to the feeling of Auld Lang Syne. Many thousands who otherwise would have sought new lands will now find it difficult to break the bonds of blood and suffering which the war has added to the usual ties binding them to the environment of their fathers.

WILL THE UNITED STATES BECOME AN EMIGRANT NATION?

The statement recently given public attention that the United States is in danger of becoming an emigrant nation should not be taken seriously. No doubt many residents of this country of foreign nativity whose kin have suffered from the privations and horrors of war may visit the place of their birth to give comfort and aid to their loved ones; but in my opinion a large majority of them will return to the places in which they have prospered. No valid foundation has been found upon which to base the radical change predicted. Such statements have encouraged plans to bring in laborers, now prohibited by law, to fill the places of those who would become part of the emigrating classes.

Without now taking up the claim that more laborers will be needed, whether or not the prediction is verified, I desire to call attention to the fact that a supply exists in abundance in Porto Rico, the Virgin Islands and the Philippines. What better way could be found to build up these possessions or what more suitable plan be devised to bind them to us to obtain their confidence, to secure their trade, and aid their development than to engage a portion of their people in our industries on the mainland? We would benefit them immensely and also avoid the reappearance of a disturbing problem that it has been our hope, from economic and other viewpoints, had been settled more than a quarter of a century ago.

SELECTED BIBLIOGRAPHY

The historical literature of the United States during World War I emphasizes diplomacy and military events taking place overseas rather than developments on the homefront. The only comprehensive general history is Frederic L. Paxson's *American Democracy and the World War*, 3 vols. (1936–1938), a useful synthesis that gives considerable attention to domestic events. An interesting anecdotal account appears in the journalist Mark Sullivan's *Our Times*, Vol. 5: *Over Here* (1933). Daniel Smith summarizes the diplomacy of the period skillfully in *The Great Departure: The United States and World War I* (1965).* For this writer's interpretation see Chapter VII of *Victory without Peace: American Foreign Relations in the Twentieth Century* (1968).* For the diplomacy of neutrality see the most recent standard account by Ernest R. May, *The World War and American Isolation*, 1914–1917 (1959),* which emphasizes the important impact of submarine warfare, and the older study stressing economic motivation by Walter Millis, *The Road to War*, 1914–1917 (1935). The diplomacy of the period when the United States was a belligerent is traced in Charles Seymour, *American Diplomacy During the World War* (1934), and David F. Trask, *The United States in the Supreme War Council: American War Aims and Inter-Allied Strategy, 1917–1918* (1961). Domestic political influences affecting the various nations at war are studied by Arno Mayer in *Political Origins of the New Diplomacy, 1917–1918* (1959).* The most recent summation of the American role in the fighting is Edward M. Coffman, *The War to End All Wars* (1968). Seward W. Livermore surveys domestic politics carefully during the period 1917–1918 and demolishes the myth of political peace at home in *Politics Is Adjourned: Woodrow Wilson and the War Congress, 1916–1918* (1966). Ruhl Bartlett has traced the development of the peace movement in *The League to Enforce Peace* (1944). Paul Birdsall's *Versailles Twenty Years After* (1941) remains the most satisfactory one-volume study of the Paris Peace Conference. Birdsall does not cover the latter months of the Paris negotiations. See David F. Trask, *General Tasker Howard Bliss and the "Sessions of the World," 1919* (1966), for this period. Arno Mayer extends his analysis of the influence of domestic politics on foreign policy

*Indicates that the work is available in a paperback edition.

to the period of the Peace Conference in *Politics and Diplomacy of Peacemaking: Containment and Counterrevolution at Versailles* (1966). President Wilson's difficulties with Congress on his return to the United States are traced in Thomas A. Bailey, *Woodrow Wilson and the Great Betrayal* (1945).* The politics of the postwar reaction are considered in Wesley M. Bagby, *The Road to Normalcy: The Presidential Campaign and Election of* 1920 (1962). The most stimulating overview of the period is found in William E. Leuchtenburg's *The Perils of Prosperity* (1958).* See also the older work of Preston W. Slosson, *The Great Crusade and After,* 1914–1928 (1930). For events of the twenties see Selig Adler, *The Isolationist Impulse: Its Twentieth-Century Reaction* (1957),* and John Braeman et al., *Change and Continuity in Twentieth-Century America: The* 1920's (1968).

For information about the wartime President students must turn to Arthur Link's extensive biography, now reaching to 1917, *Wilson,* 5 vols. (1947-   ). Two other useful works by the same author are *Woodrow Wilson and the Progressive Era,* 1910–1917 (1954),* and *Wilson the Diplomatist: A Look at His Major Policies* (1957).* The older multi-volume biography by Ray Stannard Baker is still of considerable value, *Woodrow Wilson, Life and Letters,* 8 vols. (1927–1938), as is the *Public Papers of Woodrow Wilson,* 6 vols. (1925–1926), edited by Baker and William E. Dodd. For more critical views of Wilson see the "realist" critique by John M. Blum, *Woodrow Wilson and the Politics of Morality* (1956),* and a radical analysis by N. Gordon Levin, *Woodrow Wilson and World Politics* (1968). The most useful memoir by a Wilsonian is *The Intimate Papers of Colonel House,* 4 vols. (1926–1928), edited by Charles Seymour. Blum has also contributed a study of Wilson's private secretary, *Joe Tumulty and the Wilson Era* (1951).

Works on mobilization are relatively numerous, although some important aspects of the episode are not well studied. For the propaganda effort see the discussion by the head of the Committee on Public Information, George Creel, entitled *How We Advertised America* (1920), and two scholarly studies: Harold D. Lasswell, *Propaganda Technique in the World War* (1927), and James R. Mock and Cedric Larson, *Words that Won the War: Story of the Committee on Public Information* (1940). W. F. Willoughby wrote *Government Organization in Wartime and After* (1919). For the story of industrial mobilization see Bernard Baruch, *American Industry and the War* (1941); Benedict Crowell and Robert F. Wilson, *How America Went to War,* 6 vols. (1921); and Grosvenor B. Clarkson, *Industrial America in the World War* (1923). For military and naval activity on the homefront see the work by the Secretary of the Navy, Josephus Daniels, *The Wilson Era,* 2 vols. (1944–1946); Daniel M. Beaver, *Newton D. Baker and the American War Ef-*

fort, 1917–1919 (1966), about the Secretary of War; and Edward M. Coffman's discussion of the army chief of staff, *The Hilt of the Sword: The Career of Peyton C. March* (1966).

For information on women see M. L. Degen, *History of the Women's Peace Party* (1939). Jane Addams' autobiography of these years is *The Second Twenty Years at Hull House* (1930). A recent biography of her is by John C. Farrell, *Beloved Lady: A History of Jane Addams' Ideas on Reform and Peace* (1967).

John Higham has provided the most stimulating account of nativist trends in *Strangers in the Land: Patterns of American Nativism,* 1860–1925, rev. ed. (1963).* For works on the German-Americans see C. J. Child, *The German-Americans in Politics,* 1914–1917 (1939), and Carl Wittke, *German-Americans and the World War* (1936). See also Joseph P. O'Grady, ed., *The Immigrants' Influence on Wilson's Peace Policies* (1967).

For studies of the Negro migration during World War I see R. H. Leavitt et al., *Negro Migration in* 1916–1917 (1919); Emmett J. Scott, *The American Negro in the World War* (1919); and L. V. Kennedy, *The Negro Peasant Turns Cityward* (1930).

For information on the food problem and the farmers see W. C. Mullendore, *History of the United States Food Administration,* 1917–1919 (1941); Herbert Hoover, *Years of Adventure,* 1874–1920 (1951), by the administrator of the Food Administration; and R. L. Morlan, *Political Prairie Fire: The Nonpartisan League,* 1915–1922 (1955), about the farm organization that crusaded for changes in agricultural policies during and after the war.

Works on American labor during the war include Samuel Gompers, *American Labor and the War* (1919), by the head of the American Federation of Labor; John Steuber, *Labor in Wartime* (1940); and G. S. Watkins, *Labor Problems and Labor Administration During the World War,* 2 vols (1920). For two useful works on the radical International Workers of the World (I.W.W.) see P. F. Brissenden, *The I.W.W.,* 2nd ed. (1920), and John S. Gambs, *The Decline of the I.W.W.* (1932).

For an intriguing work in intellectual history see Henry F. May, *The End of American Innocence: A Study of the First Years of Our Own Time,* 1912–1917 (1959),* which elaborates the view that "modernity" arrived just before rather than just after the war, as is argued in the introduction to this collection. Two books dealing with the ideas and activities of the Progressives are David W. Noble, *The Paradox of Progressive Thought* (1958), and Charles Forcey, *The Crossroads of Liberalism: Croly, Weyl, Lippmann, and the Progressive Era,* 1900–1925 (1961).

Among works on the challenge to civil liberties during the war years the following are particularly useful: H. C. Peterson and G. C. Fite,

Opponents of War: 1917–1918 (1957) ; Norman Thomas, *The Conscientious Objector* (1923) ; Wilbur Preston, *Aliens and Dissenters: Federal Suppression of Radicals,* 1903–1933 (1963) ; Zechariah Chafee, Jr., *Free Speech in the United States* (1941) ; R. K. Murray, *Red Scare: A Study in National Hysteria,* 1919–1920 (1955) ; and Donald Johnson, *The Challenge to American Freedoms: World War I and the Rise of the American Civil Liberties Union* (1963).

On education and religion consult L. P. Todd, *Wartime Relations of the Federal Government and the Public Schools,* 1917–1918 (1945) ; P. R. Kolbe, *The Colleges in Wartime and After* (1919) ; and R. H. Abrams, *Preachers Present Arms: A Study of the Attitudes and Activities of the Churches and Clergy in the United States,* 1914–1918 (1933).